Projects Inspired
Poetry and Ar

Céline George and Rebecca Bruce

Acknowledgements

The authors and publishers would like to thank the children at Hilden Grange School for their wonderful work in Poetry and Art.

They are also very grateful to the following teachers for their expertise and practical help: Ena Isles, Lucy Chaplin, Ann Fowler, Charlotte Parker, Karen Barclay, Susan Spence, Abby Settle and Jill Withers. A special thank you to Thérèse Dawson, Dianne Dartnell, Rosemary Jubber and John Withers for their enthusiastic support.

The authors and publishers would like to thank these artists who contributed their ideas and artwork for this project: Denis Kenny, Lorena Carbajal, Mikey Watts, Rose Rafferty, Liz Chapman, Agnes Treherne and Jo de Pear. They would like to thank Louisa Bowles from Hawkins\Brown Architects for her professional contribution to the project. A special thank you to these poets who composed poems especially for the book: Annie Freud, Michelle Lovric, Gareth P. Jones, Gavin Bruce, Mara Bergman and Jonathan Gambier.

Finally, they would like to thank Sara-Jayne White for her creative inspiration and expert help.

Céline George and Rebecca Bruce

Published by Collins
An imprint of HarperCollins*Publishers*
77–85 Fulham Palace Road
Hammersmith
London
W6 8JB

© HarperCollins*Publishers* Limited 2013

10 9 8 7 6 5 4 3 2 1

ISBN 978-0-00-750158-8

British Library Cataloguing in Publication Data
A Catalogue record for this publication is available from the British Library

Cover and internal design by Steve Evans Design and Illustration
Edited by Liz Miles
Proofread by Ros and Chris Davies
Photography by Elmcroft Studios
Photo, p69: Shutterstock

Printed and bound by Printing Express Limited, Hong Kong

We are grateful to the following for permission to reproduce copyright material:
Debjani Chatterjee for 'My Sari' from *Unzip Your Lips: 100 Poems to Read Aloud*, edited by Paul Cookson, Macmillan Children's Books 1999; Trevor Harvey for 'The Painting Lesson', © Trevor Harvey, first published in *Children's Poems*, Usborne 1990 and reproduced by permission of the poet; Nash Pollock Publishing for excerpt from 'The Tree in Season' by Robert Fisher, from *First Poems for Thinking* by Robert Fisher (Nash Pollock Publishing, 2000). 'First Day at School' by Roger Mcgough from *In the Glassroom* (© Roger McGough 1976) is printed by permission of United Agents (www.unitedagents.co.uk) on behalf of Roger McGough.

Browse the complete Collins catalogue at www.collinseducation.com

MIX
Paper from responsible sources

FSC
www.fsc.org
FSC™ C007454

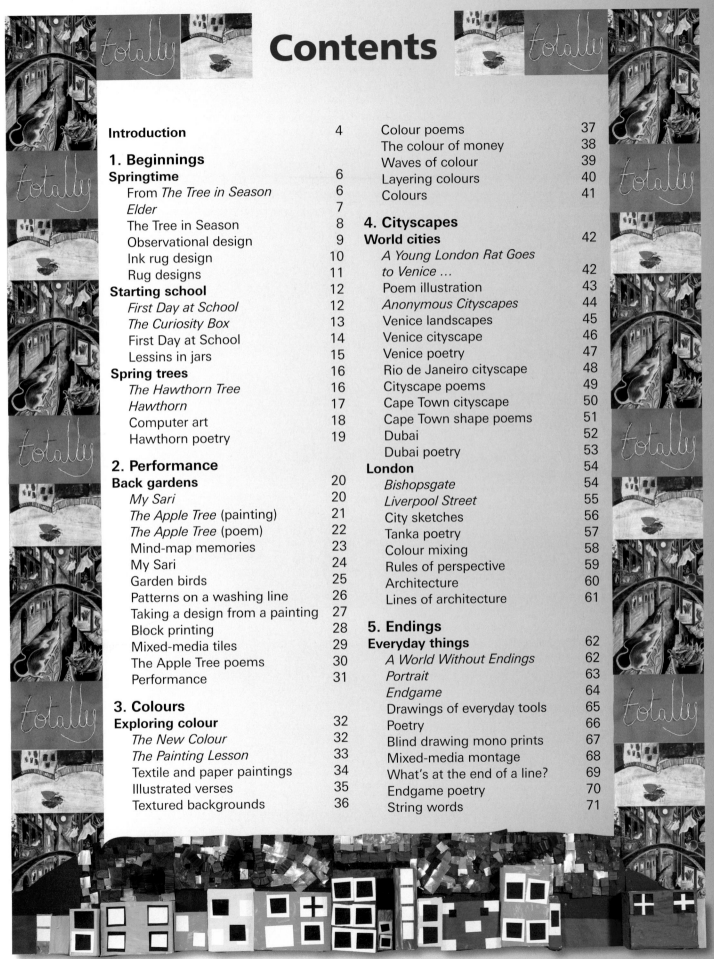

Contents

Introduction	4
1. Beginnings	
Springtime	
From *The Tree in Season*	6
Elder	7
The Tree in Season	8
Observational design	9
Ink rug design	10
Rug designs	11
Starting school	12
First Day at School	12
The Curiosity Box	13
First Day at School	14
Lessins in jars	15
Spring trees	16
The Hawthorn Tree	16
Hawthorn	17
Computer art	18
Hawthorn poetry	19
2. Performance	
Back gardens	20
My Sari	20
The Apple Tree (painting)	21
The Apple Tree (poem)	22
Mind-map memories	23
My Sari	24
Garden birds	25
Patterns on a washing line	26
Taking a design from a painting	27
Block printing	28
Mixed-media tiles	29
The Apple Tree poems	30
Performance	31
3. Colours	
Exploring colour	32
The New Colour	32
The Painting Lesson	33
Textile and paper paintings	34
Illustrated verses	35
Textured backgrounds	36

Colour poems	37
The colour of money	38
Waves of colour	39
Layering colours	40
Colours	41
4. Cityscapes	
World cities	42
A Young London Rat Goes to Venice …	42
Poem illustration	43
Anonymous Cityscapes	44
Venice landscapes	45
Venice cityscape	46
Venice poetry	47
Rio de Janeiro cityscape	48
Cityscape poems	49
Cape Town cityscape	50
Cape Town shape poems	51
Dubai	52
Dubai poetry	53
London	54
Bishopsgate	54
Liverpool Street	55
City sketches	56
Tanka poetry	57
Colour mixing	58
Rules of perspective	59
Architecture	60
Lines of architecture	61
5. Endings	
Everyday things	62
A World Without Endings	62
Portrait	63
Endgame	64
Drawings of everyday tools	65
Poetry	66
Blind drawing mono prints	67
Mixed-media montage	68
What's at the end of a line?	69
Endgame poetry	70
String words	71

Introduction

Projects Inspired by Poetry and Art offers inspirational ideas for teaching. The book is divided into five main themes and each one contains two or three poems linked closely with artworks. All the themes include poems for younger and older children and we have showcased ideas for writing, performing and displaying poetry. Each theme is presented as a project where the process is every bit as important as the final pieces of work.

Throughout the book we have included several paintings, rug designs, a print, an art installation, textile paintings and an illustration as starting points. Visiting galleries, inviting poets, artists and architects into school is always enriching and we have included quotations from some of the poets and artists who have worked closely with us. Their input has made all the difference to this exciting project.

The chapters

Each chapter begins with a poem that is linked to a piece of artwork. These poems and artworks can be used as starting points for whole class discussion prior to commencing a project. Projects are designed to be suitable for whole-class or group work.

1. Beginnings

This chapter uses the theme of new beginnings as its inspiration for artwork. There are three sections, each starting with a new poem and a new artwork. Projects include drawing from observation, followed by making ink paintings then creating a design for a contemporary rug. Children also work on computers to create images and, using the work of an installation artist as an inspiration, produce 3D artwork for an effective display.

2. Performance

This chapter is all about using colourful patterns, magical displays and eye-catching artwork to create a backdrop for performance. The theme of performance encourages children to explore their own ideas. The inspiration for the artwork is a vibrant painting based on a garden view; two wonderful poems capture perfectly the mood of the painting.

Artwork includes 3D work, creating Indian repeat patterns, block printing and making decorative tiles for display. We offer ideas about how to use artwork to enhance any poetry performance.

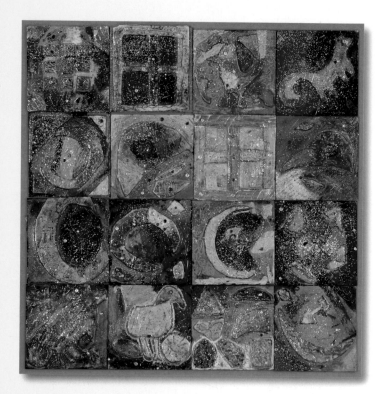

3. Colours

In this chapter, two poems are linked with colourful artworks by a practising artist, as starting points. Design work and layering colour and texture are used to create eye-catching displays. The focus is on using children's Ideas Books to collect images, text and illustrations. In this way, children will begin to gain an understanding of the workings of a real artist. Children's artwork and poetry writing is enhanced by discussing and looking at the style and approach used by the artists.

4. Cityscapes

This chapter offers two inspiring poems linked with vibrant and eye-catching cityscape paintings as starting points. Creating exciting displays of different cities enhances children's understanding of different types of city architecture, and why cities have changed. Why does Dubai have so many skyscrapers? Why are there so many bridges in Venice? Why is the City of London a mixture of ancient and modern buildings?

The chapter includes ideas for sketching buildings, colour mixing, learning about perspective and producing large architectural style paintings to reflect the towering buildings in the City of London.

Children can focus in greater detail on one cityscape, or prepare different contrasting displays.

5. Endings

In this chapter, the theme of Endings is explored through two poems and the work of an artist who uses everyday objects to represent portraits. The emotive subject of mortality is sensitively approached by focusing on visual themes that symbolise Endings. Artwork involves drawing, painting using mixed media and creating imaginative artworks linked with poetry.

Céline George and Rebecca Bruce

1. Beginnings

Springtime

There are three sections to this chapter, all closely linked to the theme of new beginnings. This first section focuses on the beauty of nature in springtime and offers an accessible approach for children.

Robert Fisher's poem, *The Tree in Season*, celebrates the beauty of a tree in springtime. The same theme is found in the work of rug maker, Denis Kenny. His rugs and wall hangings bring colour, texture, warmth and energy to their space and for Denis Kenny, the *Elder* rug design shown opposite suggests the primitive energy of springtime, with all its hope and promise.

from **The Tree in Season**

The tree hums quietly to itself

a lullaby to the buds

bursting with baby leaves

its branches ride the winds

and in all its new green glory

the tree begins to sing

Robert Fisher

Elder

Denis Kenny has collaborated with the textile artist, Brigitta Varadi, on a series of projects, one of which is this *Elder* design.

Like Denis Kenny, Brigitta Varadi looks for beauty, rhythm and pattern in her surroundings. This rug design appealed particularly to Kenny because it is clean, simple and striking with its use of colours.

The Tree in Season

Before moving on to the first part of the artwork project, leading towards a rug design, the children explore the theme of the poem *The Tree in Season* (page 6) and create their own haiku poems.

In *The Tree in Season*, the poet's use of personification in the first two lines suggests that the tree is almost like a mother, singing softly to her newborn child. Explain to the children that they will be considering this technique when writing their own poems about elder trees.

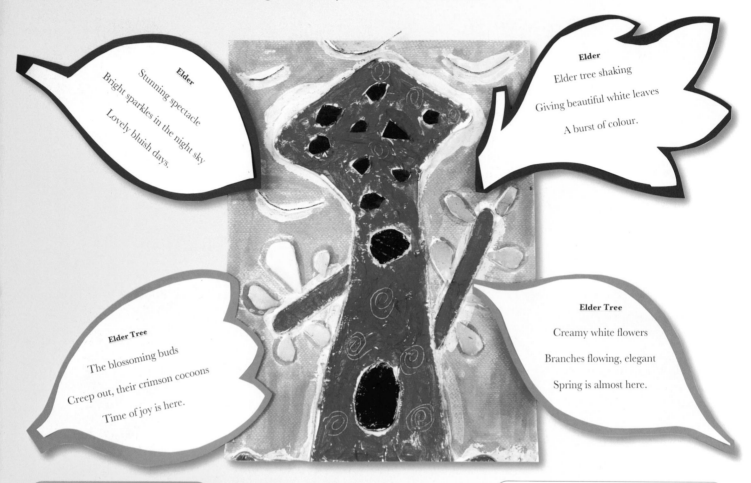

Elder

Stunning spectacle
Bright sparkles in the night sky
Lovely bluish days.

Elder

Elder tree shaking
Giving beautiful white leaves
A burst of colour.

Elder Tree

The blossoming buds
Creep out, their crimson cocoons
Time of joy is here.

Elder Tree

Creamy white flowers
Branches flowing, elegant
Spring is almost here.

Approach

1   Read the first verse of the poem, *The Tree in Season*, with the children and discuss the poet's use of personification.

2   Ask the following questions: *What is a lullaby? Who often sings a lullaby? What is the tone of the poem? In which lines does the poet use personification and what effect does it have?*

3   Discuss with the children the link between the poem and the rug design (both celebrate new beginnings in nature).

4   For inspiration pick out words from the poem and then create a simple image of a tree portraying the essence of spring.

5   Explain that you want the children to write a haiku poem about elder trees as a gift for someone in their family.

6   Give children the opportunity to write, redraft, discuss, perform and record their poems. They can recite them too, after learning them by heart.

7   Prepare the poems for display with their tree images.

Resources

- Copies of *The Tree in Season* poem
- *Elder* design image
- A4 paper
- Pencils
- Selection of painting materials
- Paint brushes
- Voice recorder

Glossary

A haiku is a Japanese form of poetry composed of three unrhymed lines with 5, 7, 5 syllables and in which every word is important. Haiku poetry is usually written in the present tense and often reflects the beauty of nature.

Observational design

The following three art exercises are all part of a process leading to the final piece of artwork in this section. Here, children will be doing their own observational drawings of natural objects.

Approach

1 Look together at the *Elder* rug (page 7) and point out its simple, strong and vibrant design. The rugs and wall hangings that Denis Kenny makes are usually the focal point in a room and can be used as a wall hanging or on the floor as a centrepiece.

2 Read the first verse of the poem *The Tree in Season* (page 6) again with the children and discuss the use of emotive language to create a strong image.

3 Give the children a selection of natural objects (e.g. leaves, feathers and shells) and ask them to draw from observation, using line only. Encourage them to look very carefully at the patterns on their object.

4 Divide an A5 sheet of paper into four sections.

5 Using their observational drawings and a viewfinder, choose four sections with interesting patterns and draw them on the A5 paper.

6 Use watercolour pencils to add colour from a limited palette, so that the patterns remain simple but striking – the same technique used in the *Elder* rug.

7 The sheet of designs can be mounted onto coloured card.

Resources
- Copy of the first verse of *The Tree in Season*
- Selection of natural objects
- A5 sketch paper
- Pencils
- Viewfinder
- Watercolour pencils
- Coloured card

Ink rug design

For the second exercise, explain to the children that they are going to use coloured inks to create some ideas of their own for rug designs.

Tell the children that Denis Kenny's rug designs are inspired by the landscape where he works and lives, with its low hills and broad, lazy rivers. He describes each rug he starts to create as being like a blank canvas.

Approach

1 Before they start work on their ink paintings, ask the children to practise first using coloured inks and brushes on large sheets of newspaper.

2 Encourage the children to use free-flowing lines and confident strokes.

3 On good-quality A5 paper, ask them to softly pencil in designs taken from their observational drawings.

4 Add extra details inspired by words from the poem, such as 'new, green glory'.

5 Using brightly-coloured ink, children can confidently fill in their designs, taking care not to blend the colours.

6 Draw a plan of a bedroom, sitting room or other domestic environment on A3 sketch paper where the rug design could be displayed.

7 Ask children to add their own rug design to the plan.

8 Display the children's rug designs as a wall hanging alongside their room plans.

Resources
- Coloured inks
- Paint brushes
- Pencils
- Sheets of newspaper
- Children's own observational designs, completed earlier
- Copy of the poem, *The Tree in Season*
- A5 and A3 sketch paper

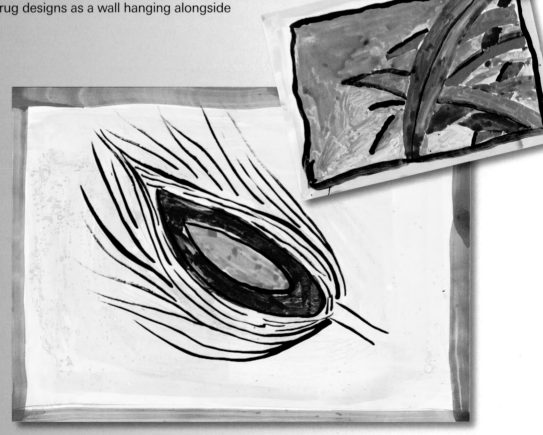

Rug designs

The last part of the process towards a final artwork involves the creation of a striking design for a contemporary rug.

Tell the children that they will be working in pairs and collaborating in a similar way to Denis Kenny and Brigitta Varadi, helping each other with ideas and inspiration. Explain that to keep their designs confident and with strong free-flowing lines, they will not be using pencils to draw with. Instead, they will be using long lengths of string to create their designs.

Approach

1   Ask the children to each choose their favourite section from their ink rug designs.

2   Use the string to create the outline of their chosen image on A3 card, helping their partner where needed.

3   Using PVA glue, fix the string in place and leave to dry.

4   Cover the surface in white tissue paper and PVA glue.

5   Use polystyrene tiles, tissue paper and extra string to build up texture and pattern in their designs.

6   Use words from the first verse of the poem, *The Tree in Season* (page 6), to inspire colour choices.

7   Use a combination of materials, including oil pastels, coloured drawing ink and acrylic paint, to build up layers of colour and texture.

8   On wet paint, use the end of a paintbrush to scratch patterns into the surface of the work.

9   Display the rug designs with some of the haiku poetry that children created earlier.

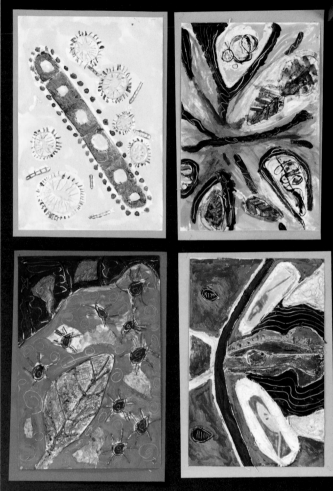

Resources
- Children's own ink rug designs, completed earlier
- Long pieces of string
- A3 card
- PVA glue
- Small pieces of white tissue paper
- Polystyrene tiles
- A copy of the first verse of the poem, *The Tree in Season*
- Oil pastels, coloured drawing ink and acrylic paint
- Paint brushes
- Haiku poetry, completed earlier

Starting school

The first day at school, which is the focus of the second section of this chapter, is a new beginning that all children will relate to. In the poem, *First Day at School*, Roger McGough recreates how bewildering it can all seem to start school for the first time. It is linked here for children's project work with Lorena Carbajal's installation *The Curiosity Box* (opposite), which comprises of objects and pictures created by children and presented as if in a museum.

First Day at School

A millionbillion miles from home
Waiting for the bell to go. (To go where?)
Why are they all so big, other children?
So noisy? So much at home they
must have been born in uniform
lived all their lives in playgrounds
Spent the years inventing games
that don't let me in. Games
that are rough, that swallow you up.

And the railings.
All around, the railings.
Are they to keep out the wolves and monsters?
Things that carry off and eat children?
Things you don't take sweets from?
Perhaps they're to stop us getting out
Running away from the lessins. Lessin.
What does a lessin look like?
Sounds small and slimy.
They keep them in glassrooms.
Whole rooms made out of glass. Imagine.
I wish I could remember my name

Mummy said it would come in useful.
Like wellies. When there's puddles.
Yellowwellies. I wish she was here.
I think my name is sewn on somewhere
Perhaps the teacher will read it for me.
Tea-cher. The one that makes the tea.

Roger McGough

The Curiosity Box

Lorena Carbajal is a visual artist who has won various awards. She has used an eclectic mixture of objects and images created by children to make her artwork installation, *The Curiosity Box*, shown here.

First Day at School

In his poem, *First Day at School* (page 12), Roger McGough uses a quirky sense of humour to create that sense of bewilderment which is common on a child's first day at school.

Having explored the poem, the children will go on to create the own installations using Lorena Carbajal's work as inspiration, and this first project will involve the children writing their own poems.

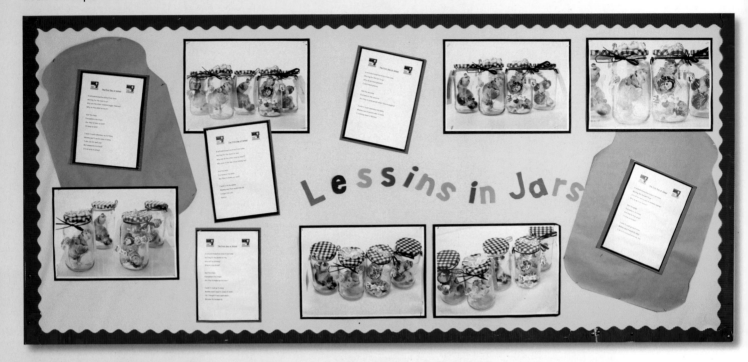

Approach

1   Explain to the children that Roger McGough has used full stops half way through some lines in the poem and these give the reader a moment to pause and think. They also add to the rhythm when reading the poem. Emphasise these points when you read the poem aloud. Point out the rhyming couplet in the last two lines and how it rounds off the poem perfectly and also makes the reader smile.

2   Discuss with the children how that first day at school can be very daunting. Explore with them their own feelings and memories of this experience.

3   Get the children to work in pairs to think of words that they have misunderstood themselves, then share their ideas with the class.

4   Ask the following questions: *Why does the child in the poem wonder where the bell is going? Why does the school have railings? What does the child in the poem think 'lessins' are? Why are the 'lessins' kept in 'glassrooms'?*

5   Using their initial ideas, ask the children to start thinking about what they might write in their own poems. Ask them to write their poems in three free verses or in stanzas with four lines in each verse. As prompts, provide a first line or two for each stanza.

6   If necessary, model poetry writing before the children begin writing their own poems.

6   Display the poems on jar-shaped mounts.

Resources
- Copies of *First Day at School* poem
- Cut-out jar shapes
- Pencils
- A4 paper
- Colouring pencils

Lessins in Jars

Remind the children how in the poem, *First Day at School* (page 12), 'lessins' sound small and slimy and are kept in 'glassrooms'. Having explored the theme of starting school through their own poetry, they are now going to create their own 'lessins' in glass jars, using Lorena Carbajal's *The Curiosity Box* (page 13) as inspiration for their own ideas.

Approach

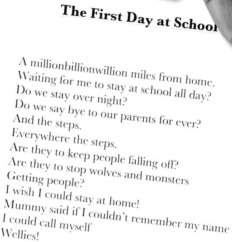

1   Read the poem, *First Day at School*, again and focus on the second verse where the poet poses the question: 'What does a 'lessin' look like?'

2   Discuss with the children what characteristics these small and slimy creatures/insects could have. What colour might they be? How many legs (if any) will they have?

3   Provide the children with Ideas Books. Ask the children to draw their own creatures into their book and add colour.

4   Look at how *The Curiosity Box* uses a collection of made objects and presents them as if in a display cabinet in a museum.

5   Working from their drawings, use thick wire and polystyrene balls to construct a simple model for their creature.

6   Use air-drying clay to add form to the model and leave to dry.

7   Colour the creature with thick marker pens and add detail with collage materials.

8   Ask the children to think of a name that describes their creature.

9   Place the creatures in plastic jars labelled with their names.

10 Display the 'Lessins in Jars' with the children's poems, created earlier, or take photographs of the artwork to create a display.

The First Day at School

A millionbillionwillion miles from home.
Waiting for me to stay at school all day?
Do we stay over night?
Do we say bye to our parents for ever?
And the steps.
Everywhere the steps.
Are they to keep people falling off?
Are they to stop wolves and monsters
Getting people?
I wish I could stay at home!
Mummy said if I couldn't remember my name
I could call myself
Wellies!

Resources

- Copy of the poem, *First Day at School*
- Image of Lorena Carbajal's *The Curiosity Box*
- Ideas Books
- Pencils
- Colouring pencils
- Thick wire
- Polystyrene balls
- Air-drying clay
- Thick marker pens in bright colours
- Collage materials
- Plastic or glass jars
- Children's poems, completed earlier

15

Spring trees

The last section in this chapter again links a spring-related poem with a rug design by Denis Kenny, this time with a hawthorn as its focus. The optimism of spring features strongly in both poem and rug design.

Jonathan Gambier's poem, *The Hawthorn Tree*, links well with Denis Kenny's rug design (opposite) as they both focus on the simple beauty of the hawthorn tree at the beginning of spring.

The Hawthorn Tree

When the harsh winter winds are over,

And my thorns, like rapiers

Have repelled their icy blast;

I will dress myself in leaves of green;

And send fragrant, white blossom

To dance like confetti at a wedding

Along hedgerows smiling at the new born sun.

Although ancient, I am once again renewed;

Till lengthening summer shadows, and the last
  blaze of autumn;

Shed my leaves once more to long winter's sleep.

Jonathan Gambier

Hawthorn

The *Hawthorn* is one of Denis Kenny's favourite designs, reflecting the beauty of nature and the optimism at the beginning of spring. It reminds him of the steely grey days in the early months of the year, with the promise of new life to come.

Computer art

Using inspiration from Jonathan Gambier's poem *The Hawthorn Tree* (page 16) and the *Hawthorn* rug (page 17) by Denis Kenny, the children are going to create a hawthorn display. Firstly, they will create their own hawthorn images using computers, then write poems based around their research into hawthorn trees to be placed alongside their art.

Artists such as David Hockney use new technology as a tool to create vibrant and expressive drawings. Explain to the children that for their first project they are going to be using computer programs to create their own images of hawthorn trees, using the *Hawthorn* rug as inspiration.

Approach

1   Look at the image of the *Hawthorn* rug and discuss its strong design; the children can use the shapes and patterns to inspire them when experimenting with their drawings.

2   Spend time on a search engine looking at relevant images of hawthorn trees in blossom.

3   Print out a few good examples for the children to use.

4   Next set up a computer program that the children are familiar with. Use the found images as visual inspiration and allow the children to experiment with techniques to create a satisfying image of a bouquet of flowers, and a hawthorn landscape.

5   If possible print the images on good quality paper and mount them on card.

6   You could have a virtual exhibition by collating their images and creating a slide show on the classroom whiteboard.

Resources
- Image of *Hawthorn* rug
- Internet access
- Printer
- Computer with suitable drawing program
- good-quality paper
- card for mounting

Hawthorn poetry

In his poem *The Hawthorn Tree* (page 16), Jonathan Gambier uses poetic language to convey his obvious delight in the start of spring and especially the light pink hawthorn blossom. He had seen Hockney's paintings of hawthorns at an exhibition and, as often happens to him as a writer, found inspiration in the use of colour and shape.

Explain to children that they are going to create their own poems inspired by both the hawthorn images they have seen and created, and Jonathan Gambier's poem.

Approach

1   Read the poem *The Hawthorn Tree* with the children and focus on the poet's use of simile and personification to create impact.

2   Working in groups of four, give the children copies of the poem. Ask them to highlight lines that show the use of personification and simile.

3   Take children outside to look at different types of trees and encourage quick sketches.

4   Ask each group to discuss answers to the following questions: *Why does the poet say that the hawthorn tree is ancient? What is the mood of the poem – celebratory, joyful, reflective? What does the poet mean by comparing the thorns to rapiers? How does the poem make you feel?* Ask the groups to feed back their answers to the rest of the class.

5   Give the children group response sheets to fill in with the following headings: Simile, Personification, Adjective, Verb and Noun, and use these to brainstorm ideas for their group poems.

6   Ask the children to write their own eight-line poems with the title The Hawthorn Tree – one per group. Hand out eight strips of paper to each group so that everyone writes two poetic lines each.

7   Ask the children to read their group poems aloud and display the poems together.

8   Present a virtual exhibition using the children's drawings and poems to create a slide show.

The Hawthorn Tree

When the long, bitter winter is over
And my thorns like sharp pins
Protect me from icy winds,
I will cover myself in dark green leaves.
And dress in white and pink
To dance like angels at a ball.
My blossoms peek out through my leaves
Along hedgerows bowing to the new born king.

Glossary

Personification: giving human qualities to a non-living thing.

Simile: a figure of speech in which two things are compared using the word 'like' or 'as'.

Resources

- The poem, *The Hawthorn Tree*
- Images of David Hockney's Hawthorn paintings
- Response sheets
- Ideas Books and sketch pencils
- Strips of paper and highlighter pens

2. Performance

Back gardens

Central to this chapter is the theme of performance. Two poems and a painting provide the inspiration for a range of artwork projects culminating in a performance of children's own poetry.

Debjani Chatterjee's *My Sari*, remembers the wonderful colours of saris hanging out in the sun to dry. The link between this poem and *The Apple Tree* painting (opposite) is that they are both set in someone's back garden. Both the poem and the painting conjure up happy and colourful images remembered in childhood.

My Sari

Saris hang on the washing line:
a rainbow in our neighbourhood.
This little orange one is mine,
it has a mango leaf design.
I wear it as a Rani would.
It wraps around me like sunshine,
it ripples silky down my spine,
and I stand tall and feel so good.

Debjani Chatterjee

The Apple Tree

In this painting, *The Apple Tree*, artist Mikey Watts has taken his inspiration from childhood memories of a tree in the back garden of the house he lived in for a number of years. He loved the tree and wanted to have a way of remembering it when he had moved from the house. He purposely kept the painting simple, so just included the tree, the patio and the fence behind the tree and then the skyline above.

This poem was inspired by Mikey Watts's painting, *The Apple Tree*. Mara Bergman has taken images from the painting as her inspiration for this poem of the same name.

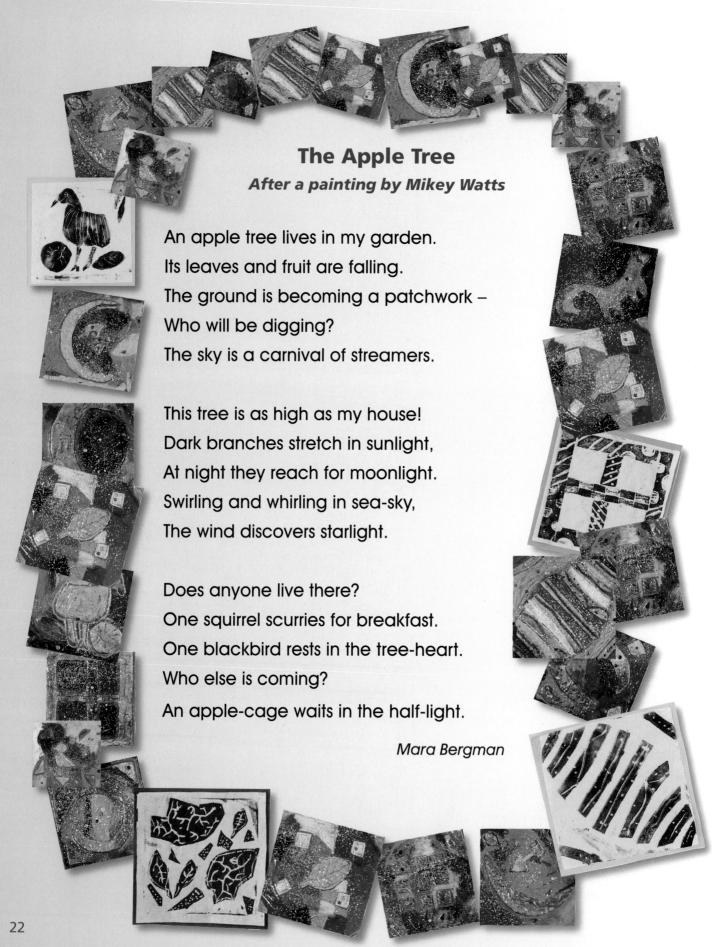

The Apple Tree
After a painting by Mikey Watts

An apple tree lives in my garden.
Its leaves and fruit are falling.
The ground is becoming a patchwork –
Who will be digging?
The sky is a carnival of streamers.

This tree is as high as my house!
Dark branches stretch in sunlight,
At night they reach for moonlight.
Swirling and whirling in sea-sky,
The wind discovers starlight.

Does anyone live there?
One squirrel scurries for breakfast.
One blackbird rests in the tree-heart.
Who else is coming?
An apple-cage waits in the half-light.

Mara Bergman

Mind-map memories

Explain to the children that they will be exploring a poem, *My Sari* (page 20), and a painting, *The Apple Tree* (page 21), and that they will be creating a mind map to record their responses.

Approach

1   Look at *The Apple Tree* painting and focus on the images the artist has included in the painting (a squirrel, a birdcage, the sun, the moon, a window and a spade).

2   Read the poem, *My Sari*, then give children a copy of it. They will look in detail at the images in the poem later. For now, focus on children's overall response; brainstorm powerful words or phrases that describe both the poem and the painting.

3   Ask the following questions: *Which images do you like the best? Where is the setting for the poem and the painting?*

4   Ask children to create a mind map in their Ideas Books, using words and pictures to convey the upbeat mood of both the poem and the painting.

Resources
- Copies of *The Apple Tree* painting by Mikey Watts
- Copies of *My Sari* poem by Debjani Chatterjee
- Ideas Books
- Sketch pencils
- Colouring pencils

23

My Sari

The children now work towards creating a class poem as a response to the poem *My Sari* (page 20) and the painting *The Apple Tree* (page 21).

Approach

1 Before reading the poem aloud, explain to the children that it has a definite rhyming pattern: ABAABAAB and this makes it flow easily when read aloud. The form of the poem is a simple one with one verse and eight short lines, with eight beats to a line.

2 Look at a selection of illustrated books that reflect other cultures and discuss their traditions with a special focus on the sort of clothes that are worn; include stories that reflect the Indian culture with a focus on saris.

3 Read the poem, *My Sari*, with the children and ask the following questions: *Why has the poet used the word 'rainbow' to describe the saris? What is the effect of that? What is a 'Rani'* (an Indian princess)? *What is a 'mango leaf design'? What is the poem about?*

4 Show the children some pictures of a mango and explain that the mango and its leaves are often used in Indian designs to reflect the beauty of nature.

5 Display a collection of vibrantly coloured materials with Indian designs to inspire the children's writing.

6 Now look again at the painting *The Apple Tree* by Mikey Watts and discuss it in terms of colour and the artist's use of different images in the composition.

7 Brainstorm some powerful rhyming words for the children to use in their own poems so that they link closely with images in the *The Apple Tree* painting.

8 Ask the children to work in pairs to explore their ideas inspired by Mikey Watts's vibrant artwork.

9 Use the children's ideas to write a class poem with the title *Rainbow Colours*, using a similar form to that of *My Sari* (eight lines and the same rhyme pattern).

10 Place the image of Mikey Watts's painting next to the children's poem in their Literacy Books.

11 Perform the poem as a class choral recital. Children could wear saris and do a simple dance routine as part of the performance.

12 Older children could write a more challenging class poem by including the same number of beats as in *My Sari*.

Resources

- Selection of books on other cultures and traditions
- Copy of *My Sari* poem by Debjani Chatterjee
- Pictures of mangoes
- Materials with Indian designs
- Copy of *The Apple Tree* painting by Mikey Watts
- Literacy Books

Garden birds

In this third project, the children are going to create some 3D work based on the painting *The Apple Tree* (page 21), to display with their class poem.

In the image of *The Apple Tree* painting there is a little bird sitting in the tree. This simple bird motif is framed in the tree's heart and it serves as a focal point for this project.

Approach

1   Prepare a bold, symmetrical template of a bird with its wings drawn separately.

2   Set out various materials for the children to use and ask them to look closely at Mikey Watts's painting, *The Apple Tree*, as their birds are going to be filled with the colours and shapes found in his artwork.

3   Spend some time decorating the bird templates with collage, pens, pastels and paints.

4   Let the children work freely and encourage them to choose their own combination of materials.

5   Do the same with the wings.

6   Let everything dry thoroughly then cut around the templates and make two slits in the side of the body for the wings.

7   Spend time adding any extra details to the birds.

8   Display the birds on a board, creating a background tree for them to be perched on, or make a small hole in their backs and hang them vertically using colourful thread.

9   Display the artwork with the class poem.

Resources
- Bird and wing templates on thin card
- Scissors
- Glue
- Collage materials
- Paints
- Pastels
- Pens
- Thread

Patterns on a washing line

Repeat patterns are a strong element in Indian designs. They are used in many ways in Indian art, as can be seen in traditional architecture, painting and textiles. By using the poem *My Sari* (page 20), by Debjani Chatterjee, the children will be able to link language with visual imagery. Using this simple method, children can experiment and create patterns of their own, which is the focus of this display project.

Approach

1   Explain to the children that the artist Mikey Watts used different types of oil pastels in his painting and then scratched the surface to reveal new colours and to define details.

2   Read the poem, *My Sari*, and explain to the children that they are going to make colourful patterned pictures for a washing line display.

3   Look at some images of Indian repeat patterns and talk about how Indian designers use these in their designs.

4   Point out the bright colours used by Mikey Watts in his painting, *The Apple Tree* (page 21). Encourage the children to use similar brightly coloured thick oil pastels to cover a sheet of A4 paper in a patchwork pattern.

5   Apply a thick layer of black acrylic paint over the whole patchwork pattern.

6   Use toothpicks to scratch a repeat pattern through the paint to reveal the oil pastel colours beneath the top, black layer.

7   Cut the patterned paper into shapes of clothes, including trousers, socks and shirts.

8   Use a washing line and clothes pegs to display the finished items of clothing.

9   Add other images taken from *The Apple Tree* painting to the display.

Resources
- Examples of Indian repeat patterns
- Copy of *The Apple Tree* painting by Mikey Watts
- Copy of *My Sari* poem by Debjani Chatterjee
- A4 paper
- Oil pastels
- Black acrylic paint
- Toothpicks
- Scissors
- Washing line and pegs

Taking a design from a painting

The children now focus in more detail on the images within Mikey Watts's painting, *The Apple Tree* (page 21). The images are all ones that he wanted to keep in his memory after he had left his childhood home. He knew the tree for many years, in all seasons, and at both day and night. That is why there is both a sun and a moon, and the colours recreate a feeling of both night and day.

Explain to the children that they are going to take an image from *The Apple Tree* painting to create their own designs. These designs will then be used later as a template for block print.

Approach

1   Discuss the different images that Mikey Watts has included in his painting in terms of colour and pattern.

2   Read Mara Bergman's poem, *The Apple Tree* (page 22), and ask the following questions: *In the first stanza, what are the images that Mara Bergman has taken directly from the painting? How tall is the apple tree in the poem? What two creatures are mentioned both in the poem and in the painting?*

3   Ask the children to choose areas of Mikey Watts's painting that they can draw, for use in their own designs. Ask them to draw them in their Ideas Books using sketch pencils.

4   Colour the drawings using black pens.

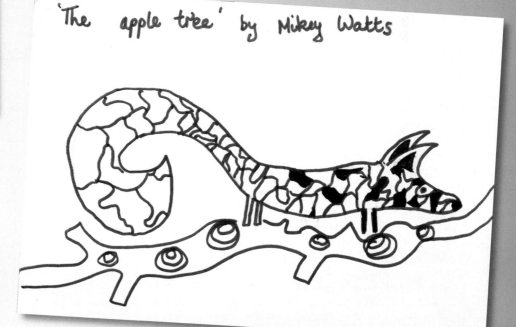

Resources
- Image of *The Apple Tree* painting by Mikey Watts
- Copy of *The Apple Tree* poem by Mara Bergman
- Sketch pencils
- Ideas Books
- Black fine-line pens

27

Block printing

Explain to the children that they are going on to make a block print of their design based on a section of *The Apple Tree* painting (page 21).

The general approach to this activity should be one of design, make and print. Their first task (page 27) was to choose an area of the painting that they could draw in their Ideas Books as their design and then to colour it in black pen. This will be the template for their block print, which is the focus of this project.

Approach

1 To make the printing block, cut the basic shape of their drawn design (see page 27) out of a polystyrene tile.

2 Stick the polystyrene shape firmly onto a backing board.

3 Using a biro, add detail by drawing into the polystyrene to create indentations.

4 Leave until completely dry.

5 Prepare a printing area with rollers, ink and a flat, easy-to-wipe surface.

6 Roller black ink evenly over the surface of the tile. The ink should only be applied to the polystyrene, not the backing board.

7 Provide a stack of a variety of papers on a clean surface for the children to use for their printing.

8 Ask the children to place a sheet of paper carefully over the top of their inked tile.

9 Smooth the paper down onto the ink with the palm of the hand, making sure you produce an even pressure to the surface.

10 Lift the paper away from the block and place the inked design on a rack to dry.

11 Once dry, neatly mount the prints on brightly-coloured card and display closely as a group.

Resources
- Ideas Books
- Pencils
- Black pens
- Polystyrene tiles
- Boards
- Biros
- PVA glue
- Black printing ink
- Rollers
- Variety of paper
- Brightly-coloured card

Mixed-media tiles

The poet Mara Bergman used Mikey Watts's *The Apple Tree* (page 21) as a focus for writing a poem that expresses bold images evoked by memory (page 22). In a similar way, the children have based their own block prints on *The Apple Tree*.

For this next project, the children will create a powerful display from their printing blocks (page 28), which can help form the backdrop for the performance they are working towards.

Approach

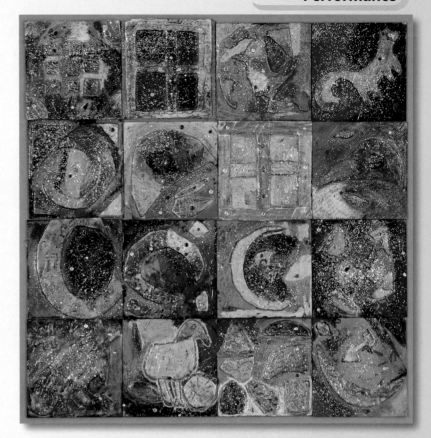

1 Read Mara Bergman's poem again as a class to inspire the children to use evocative colours to transform their printing blocks (page 28) into a poetry and art patchwork.

2 Using the washed, dry printing blocks, children should start to layer vibrant oil pastels over the blocks.

3 Encourage children to use the colours in Mikey Watts's painting as an inspiration, blending and layering as they work.

4 Once the whole printing block is covered with oil pastels, thickly paint a layer of PVA glue over the whole surface.

5 Use the wrong end of a brush to draw patterns in the surface. Make sure this is done while the glue is still wet.

6 Place sequins and glitter on the glued surface, being careful to use them sparingly.

7 Leave the tiles to dry.

8 Ask the children to draw, write and collage parts of Mara Bergman's poem on extra tiles. These will form part of the display.

Resources

- Copies of *The Apple Tree* poem by Mara Bergman
- Copy of *The Apple Tree* painting by Mikey Watts
- Printing blocks
- Oil pastels
- PVA glue
- Paint brushes
- Glitter
- Sequins

The Apple Tree poems

Explain to the children that Mara Bergman has created a poem that links seamlessly with Mikey Watts's painting, *The Apple Tree* (page 21). She uses personification and simile to convey the powerful presence of the apple tree. In the second stanza, she conveys the contrasting ways in which the apple tree's branches move during the day and night.

Explain to the children that they are going to explore Mara Bergman's poem *The Apple Tree* (page 22), looking at how she uses language to create an image of the tree in their minds. They will go on to draft their own poems about a tree, inspired by Mara Bergman's use of language.

Approach

1 Read *The Apple Tree* by Mara Bergman to the children.

2 Pose the following quick-fire questions and ask the children to respond using whiteboards: *What figure of speech is used in the first line of the poem? In the second stanza, what figure of speech is used to describe the size of the tree? In the third stanza, the poet tells us that some animals live in the apple tree. What are they? Which line in the poem hints at the season of the year?*

3 Look at Mikey Watts's painting, *The Apple Tree*, and ask the children to explore their own ideas using memory to evoke an image of a tree, perhaps in their own gardens. Ask them to describe the tree in terms of colour, shape and setting.

4 Working with response partners, ask children to start drafting their own cinquain poems using the title, *A Tree in My Garden*, and encourage them to use adventurous vocabulary.

5 Encourage children to learn their cinquain poems by heart. Provide an opportunity for the children to recite them.

6 Prepare children for performing a choral recital of Mara Bergman's poem, *The Apple Tree*, to an audience.

Resources
- Copies of *The Apple Tree* poem by Mara Bergman
- Copy of *The Apple Tree* painting by Mikey Watts
- Drafting books and pencils
- Whiteboards, pens and pencils

Glossary

Cinquain: a short five-lined poem with twenty-two syllables: 2, 4, 6, 8 and 2. The lines can run on and it is often better if they do. The last line with only two syllables needs to make a real impact.

Personification: giving human qualities to a non-living thing.

Simile: a figure of speech in which two things are compared using the word 'like' or 'as'.

Stanza: Two or more lines of poetry that together form one of the divisions of the poem.

Performance

The culmination of the project work in this chapter is the children's performance of their poetry.

To enhance any poetry performance, it is important to set the scene by using music, costumes and dance to bring a poem to life and to engage and entertain the audience.

Approach

1   Choreograph some simple dance routines for the children to perform to an audience, using an Indian theme.

2   Encourage children to memorise their class poem, *Rainbow Colours* (see page 24), in preparation for performance.

3   Practise reading the poem, *My Sari* by Debjani Chatterjee (page 20) in groups, and the class poem, *Rainbow Colours*, in preparation for performance.

4   Hold the music, dance and poetry performance.

5   Play some Indian music as the audience arrives.

6   Older children can prepare their own slide presentation using images of their artwork with words taken from their poems. They can include a piece of music of their choice.

7   Give children the opportunity to share their slide presentation with a group, perhaps starting it with a reading of *The Apple Tree* (page 22) by Mara Bergman to set the scene.

Resources
- Indian music
- Copy of *My Sari* poem by Debjani Chatterjee
- Children's poems
- Indian costumes
- Copy of *The Apple Tree* poem by Mara Bergman
- Copy of the class poem, *Rainbow Colours*
- Computer with a presentation program

3. Colours
Exploring colour

In this chapter, two poems have been linked with an artist's work, all on the topic of colour. Read the poetry with the children first, look at the paintings on page 34 and then encourage them to write their own poems.

The poems, *The New Colour* and *The Painting Lesson*, together with Rose Rafferty's paintings, convey to the children how the use of colour influences the way they see the world. Colour can evoke an atmosphere whether through a poem or a work of art.

The New Colour

'It isn't quite red,'
Billy Young said,
'but nor is it orange or pink.
It's kind of like blue,
with a purplish hue.
Alfie, what do you think?'

'It reminds me of grey,'
replied Alfie Bray.
Ashna said, 'I'd call it mauve.'
'I don't think it's either,'
said Richie McGiver,
'or maybe a little of both.'

'It reminds me of green,'
said Stevie McQueen,
'like that of a leaf on a tree.'
'It's not unlike white,'
stated Christopher Blight.
But it looked more like black to me.

The class gathered round,
saying blue, black and brown,
some saying violet or puce.
Mrs Bruce raided her voice
And gave us the choice,
'Calm down or detention. You choose!'

'What's all this fuss?'
She asked all of us.
'I'm feeling quite disappointed.'
The whole class dispersed,
And, as though they'd rehearsed,
Everyone turned and pointed.

When she saw what I'd mixed
Her expression was fixed
Her eyes looked glazed and all funny.
'If we could make more,
we would never be poor.
This is the colour of money.'

'What did you use?'
asked Mrs Bruce.
'Surely you must recall.'
'I was too busy stirring,
to see it occurring,
I think I used them all.'

But she wouldn't take no
For an answer, and so
She grabbed some green and squeezed.
It landed on mine
And in barely no time
It looked like someone had sneezed.

Gareth P Jones

This poem, *The Painting Lesson* by Trevor Harvey, links well with Rose Rafferty's work on the next page, as both convey the importance of colours and how colours can remind us of people or places.

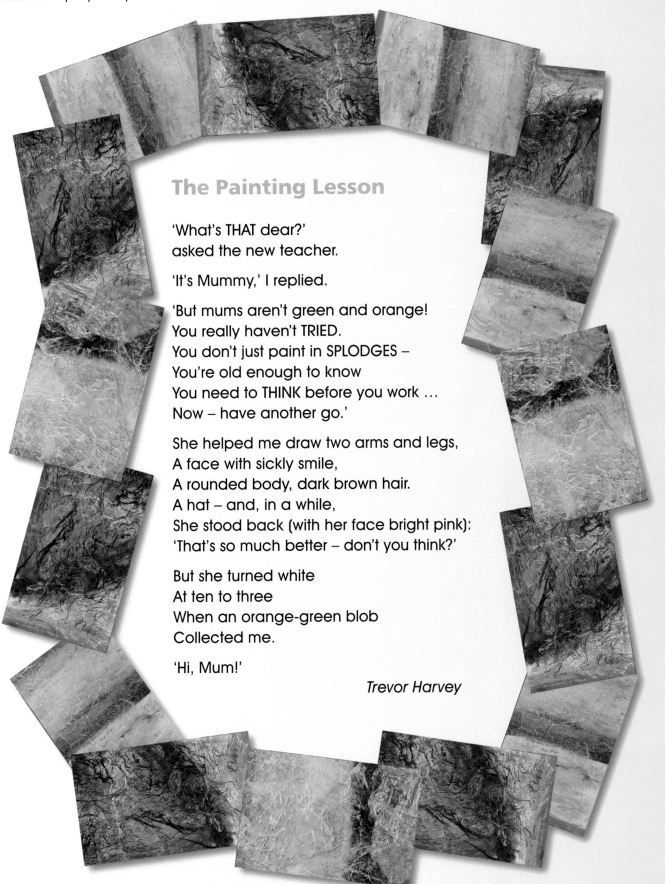

The Painting Lesson

'What's THAT dear?'
asked the new teacher.

'It's Mummy,' I replied.

'But mums aren't green and orange!
You really haven't TRIED.
You don't just paint in SPLODGES –
You're old enough to know
You need to THINK before you work …
Now – have another go.'

She helped me draw two arms and legs,
A face with sickly smile,
A rounded body, dark brown hair.
A hat – and, in a while,
She stood back (with her face bright pink):
'That's so much better – don't you think?'

But she turned white
At ten to three
When an orange-green blob
Collected me.

'Hi, Mum!'

Trevor Harvey

Textile and paper paintings

Two of Rose Rafferty's artworks are shown here – one is a textile painting using hot colours and in the other the artist has used cool-coloured, torn papers.

Illustrated verses

A key focus of this project is on children using Ideas Books to collect images, text and illustration.

Explain to the children that the artist Rose Rafferty stresses the importance of keeping a journal or Ideas Book to collect images and objects, then to write about why you have collected them, so that your text and the images are kept together. (An Ideas Book is a helpful planning tool for teachers, too. Use it to keep a visual record of ideas and materials for inspiration.)

The humorous narrative poem by Gareth P Jones, *The New Colour* (page 32), has a definite rhyming pattern that carries a natural lightness and humour (similar to that of a limerick). The rhyming pattern is: AABCCB. The poem has a clear rhythm, or beat, and this is especially effective when read aloud.

Approach

1   Read the poem, *The New Colour*, to the children and ask them to close their eyes and create a picture in their minds.

2   Discuss what the poem is about and how the teacher, Mrs Bruce, wrecked the colour in the end. Pose the following questions: *What were the children talking about in the poem before their teacher joined in? Why does their teacher think that the new colour is the colour of money? Did Mrs Bruce manage to make the colour again? What is the rhyming pattern?*

3   Give a copy of the poem to the children and ask them to circle one or two verses, cut them out and stick each one on a separate page in the middle of their Ideas Books.

5   Encourage the children to illustrate each verse with pictures to describe it.

Resources
- Copies of *The New Colour* poem by Gareth P Jones
- Ideas Books
- Scissors
- Pencils
- Glue
- Colouring pencils

Textured backgrounds

Explain to the children that they are going to make textured background paintings using oil pastels in hot colours with a small amount of purple.

Together, look at Rose Rafferty's use of hot colours in her textile painting (page 34, top). The artist chose hot reds, oranges and purples to evoke the city of Venice with its perfect sunsets.

Approach

1   Place sugar paper on tables and put thick portrait card on top of the sugar paper.

2   Display a list of hot colours, including purple, in the classroom.

3   Ask the children to choose one colour from the list and make a thick line along the top of the card with the oil pastel.

4   Choose another colour and blend with the first colour. Continue blending and smudging different colours until the card is completely covered.

5   To create a textured surface on the card, scrunch up some tissue paper, unwrap and tear. Using watered down PVA glue and a brush, stick the tissue paper onto the card and leave to dry.

6   Encourage the children to use their fingers to apply very small amounts of metallic poster paint as highlights on the textured surface.

7   Ask the children to choose a favourite section on their textured background card, then to turn it over and draw a rectangular shape around it using a ruler. Make sure all the children's shapes are the same size.

8   Cut out the square neatly and place under a cut-out card mount.

9   Display the paintings somewhere visible in the school, perhaps the library, so everyone has a chance to see them.

Resources
- Copy of Rose Rafferty's artwork in hot colours
- A2 sugar paper
- A4 thick card
- Oil pastels
- Pale pink, pale blue and white tissue paper
- PVA glue
- Paint brushes
- Metallic poster paint
- Pencils
- Rulers
- Scissors or paper cutter
- Cut-out card mounts

Colour poems

Explain to the children that they are going to look in more detail at *The New Colour* (page 32), and then work together to write a new first verse for it. They will also use their textured paintings (page 36) as inspiration.

Emphasise to them that when writing poetry it is important to redraft work several times, so if they do this they are working like a real poet.

Approach

1   Read the poem, *The New Colour*, again with the children.

2   Encourage the children to share and explore their ideas, referring to the illustrated verses already completed in their Ideas Books.

3   Focus on the first verse of the poem and discuss its rhyming pattern (AABCCB) and the rhythm/beat. (For older children it is useful to count the number of syllables in each line to help with the beat.)

4   Look at the children's textured paintings for inspiration and discuss how different layers of colour were used to achieve the final piece of artwork.

5   Brainstorm and display a list of colour names that children could use in their verses.

6   Working in small groups, ask the children to compose a new first verse for the poem. Encourage them to use the same rhyming pattern and beat as Gareth's poem.

7   Give the children the chance to redraft their verses over a few lessons.

8   Create a display of children's verses with their textured background paintings.

The New Colour

'I don't think it's red,'
said Jessica Bread.
'But nor is it pink or lemon.'
'It has to be puce,'
remarked Mrs Bruce.
'But it could be melon.'

Resources

- Copies of *The New Colour* poem by Gareth P Jones
- A copy of Rose Rafferty's artwork, using hot colours
- Ideas Books
- Textured background paintings
- List of colour names
- A3 paper for drafting
- Pencils

The colour of money

Continuing with the children's project work on colour, revisit the poem, *The New Colour* (page 32), and look in particular at how the poet refers to the colour of money. Tell the children that they are going to design their own banknotes for an imaginary land.

Approach

1 Show the children an image of a banknote and discuss it in terms of its design details such as its value, colour and pictures. Explain that for their banknotes, they are going to use symmetrical designs and whatever is on one side must also be on the other. (The Bank of England has a very useful website with resources that may inspire children's designs.)

2 Ask children to focus on a place, hobby or activity that is special to them and choose an image to use as part of their design. Ask questions such as: *Do you like collecting things? What things reflect your personality?*

3 Encourage the children to draw the outline of a banknote in their Ideas Books, and to sketch their designs using their initial ideas on one side of the shape.

4 Hand out A3 banknote (rectangular) templates. The children draw their original design in pencil on one side only of the rectangle.

5 Take a sheet of tracing paper and trace the design with a pencil. Flip the tracing paper over onto the opposite side of the note and draw over the pencil lines again to create a symmetrical design.

6 Draw over the design with a fine-line pen.

7 Create a display that links the banknotes closely with the poem.

Resources
- Sketch pencils
- Fine-line pens
- Copies of *The New Colour* poem by Gareth P Jones
- Tracing paper
- A3 rectangular paper banknote templates

Waves of colour

In Gareth P Jones's poem, *The New Colour* (page 32), he talks about the process of colour-mixing and how something magical can occur when you least expect it. Having used Rose Rafferty's textile painting to inspire their own work, the children are now going to layer and blend colours to create a sea effect.

Approach

1 Look at Rose Rafferty's torn-paper painting (page 34, bottom) and discuss the way she blends colours to create new ones. Explain to the children that in this painting Rose Rafferty has used cool colours to create a seascape.

2 For a similar effect soak watercolour paper with water using a brush.

3 Use wet watercolour paint to build up tones of colour using the paler colours first. Allow the paint to spread naturally to create exciting colour effects.

4 Add richer colours to parts of the paper.

5 Flick dry, white powder paint sparingly onto the painting to create a sea spray effect. The key to the success of these paintings is to know when to stop.

6 Place the paintings in a mount and display.

Resources

- Palette of watercolours
- A4 watercolour paper
- Medium-sized soft brushes
- Water pots
- White powder paint
- Mounts

Layering colours

Explain to children that, for their final project, they are going to create a display that links artwork and poetry, on the theme of colour.

They start here by creating an artwork background for the display. The technique of layering colours can be used successfully in any display and creates a very effective background design.

Approach

1   Read the poem *The Painting Lesson* (page 33) and link the colourful description of the child's mother with the vibrant colours used in Rose Rafferty's paintings (page 34).

2   Cut out strips of tissue paper using hot colours plus a strip of purple.

3   Give children A4 card, and starting with the palest colours, stick the tissue strips from the top of the card using glue liberally.

4   Begin to layer deeper colours over the surface, making sure that they remain in a horizontal position.

5   Create a shiny, solid surface by coating the work with PVA glue and leaving to dry.

Resources

- Copies of *The Painting Lesson* poem by Trevor Harvey
- Copies of Rose Rafferty's paintings
- A4 card
- Strips of tissue paper in hot colours
- Strips of tissue paper in purple
- PVA glue
- Glue brushes

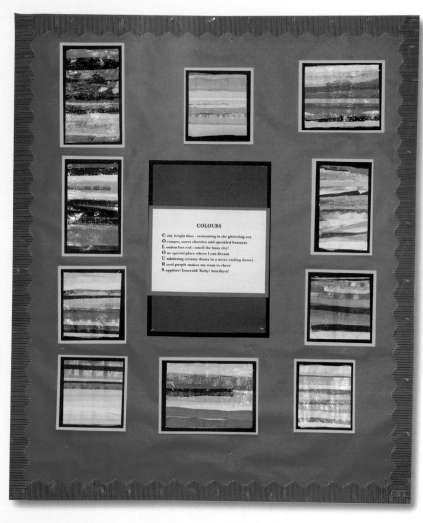

Colours

Share the poem *The Painting Lesson* (page 33) with the children again. Explain how the poet Trevor Harvey has written key words in capital letters to emphasise the teacher's harsh response to the child's drawing. This first part of the poem is written in the form of a dialogue between the child and the teacher; the rest of the poem is in the voice of the child. The mood changes from being quite serious to being surprisingly upbeat and ends on an unexpected note, making the reader smile.

The children are now going to use inspiration from Trevor Harvey's poem to create acrostic poems to go on their 'Colour' display with their layered colour artwork.

Approach

1   Read the poem, *The Painting Lesson*, aloud and focus on the poet's use of dialogue to convey the feelings of the child and the teacher.

2   Ask the following questions: *How did the new teacher react to the child's drawing at the beginning of the poem? How do you think the child felt when the teacher wasn't pleased with his drawing? Why did the teacher help the child to do another drawing? Why did the teacher turn white at the end of the poem?*

3   Now look again at Rose Rafferty's colourful textile and torn-paper paintings. Discuss the colour contrast between the two pieces and ask the children to think about words that express those colours.

4   Using the word COLOURS, ask the children to compose a class acrostic poem (where the first letter of each line together make a word, as in the example on the right).

5   Encourage the children to share their ideas by writing their lines of poetry on separate strips of paper. Arrange the lines to create the most effective acrostic poem.

6   Display the poem with the layered-colours artwork. When children are writing group poems or class poems, giving each child a strip of paper to use for their writing ensures that each child's idea is read aloud and placed somewhere in the poem. This approach is useful when writing any poem collaboratively.

COLOURS

C old, bright blue - swimming in the glittering sea
O ranges, sweet cherries and speckled bananas
L ondon bus red - smell the busy city!
O ne special place where I can dream
U ndulating creamy dunes in a never ending desert
R oyal purple makes me want to cheer
S apphire! Emerald! Ruby! Amethyst!

Resources
- Copies of *The Painting Lesson* poem by Trevor Harvey
- Images of Rose Rafferty's two artworks
- Strips of paper
- Pencils
- Layering colours artwork

4. Cityscapes

World cities

This chapter takes you and your class on a journey to different cities around the world – Venice, Rio de Janeiro, Cape Town and Dubai. For the following nine projects, children will be exploring two poems and a set of paintings.

Michelle Lovric often uses Venice as a setting for her fiction, and in her narrative poem, *A Young London Rat Goes to Venice …*, Venice is the chosen location, too. This poem, Agnes Treherne's painting (opposite) and Liz Chapman's *Anonymous Cityscapes* paintings (page 44) evoke the essence of city life, with its exuberant colours and majestic architecture.

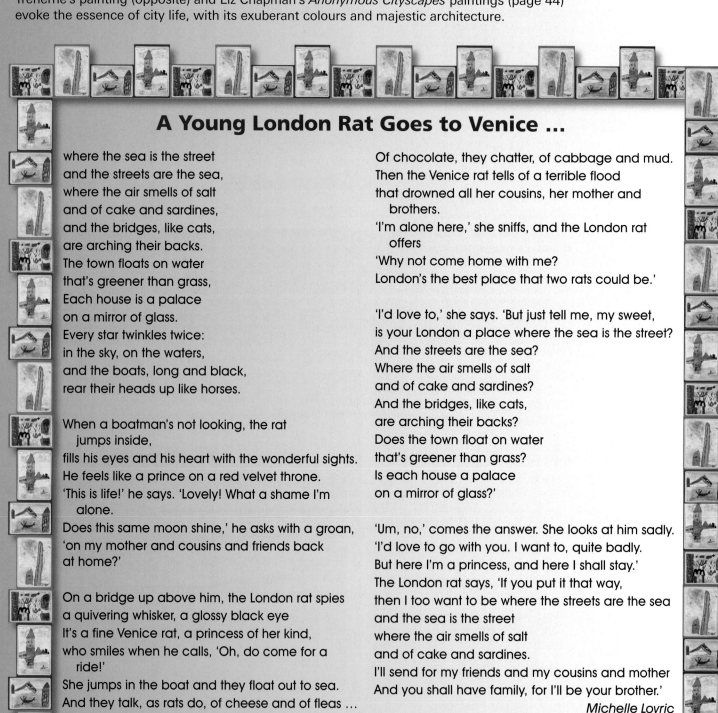

A Young London Rat Goes to Venice …

where the sea is the street
and the streets are the sea,
where the air smells of salt
and of cake and sardines,
and the bridges, like cats,
are arching their backs.
The town floats on water
that's greener than grass,
Each house is a palace
on a mirror of glass.
Every star twinkles twice:
in the sky, on the waters,
and the boats, long and black,
rear their heads up like horses.

When a boatman's not looking, the rat
   jumps inside,
fills his eyes and his heart with the wonderful sights.
He feels like a prince on a red velvet throne.
'This is life!' he says. 'Lovely! What a shame I'm
   alone.
Does this same moon shine,' he asks with a groan,
'on my mother and cousins and friends back
at home?'

On a bridge up above him, the London rat spies
a quivering whisker, a glossy black eye
It's a fine Venice rat, a princess of her kind,
who smiles when he calls, 'Oh, do come for a
   ride!'
She jumps in the boat and they float out to sea.
And they talk, as rats do, of cheese and of fleas …

Of chocolate, they chatter, of cabbage and mud.
Then the Venice rat tells of a terrible flood
that drowned all her cousins, her mother and
   brothers.
'I'm alone here,' she sniffs, and the London rat
   offers
'Why not come home with me?
London's the best place that two rats could be.'

'I'd love to,' she says. 'But just tell me, my sweet,
is your London a place where the sea is the street?
And the streets are the sea?
Where the air smells of salt
and of cake and sardines?
And the bridges, like cats,
are arching their backs?
Does the town float on water
that's greener than grass?
Is each house a palace
on a mirror of glass?'

'Um, no,' comes the answer. She looks at him sadly.
'I'd love to go with you. I want to, quite badly.
But here I'm a princess, and here I shall stay.'
The London rat says, 'If you put it that way,
then I too want to be where the streets are the sea
and the sea is the street
where the air smells of salt
and of cake and sardines.
I'll send for my friends and my cousins and mother
And you shall have family, for I'll be your brother.'

Michelle Lovric

Poem illustration

Agnes Treherne was inspired by Michelle Lovric's poem (opposite) when producing this painting. She believes such images should be exciting and intriguing to inspire children to read the poem that they are illustrating – like windows into poems that give a glimpse of what lies beyond the page.

Anonymous Cityscapes

Artist Liz Chapman's work includes a set of paintings called *Anonymous Cityscapes*, a selection of which are shown here.

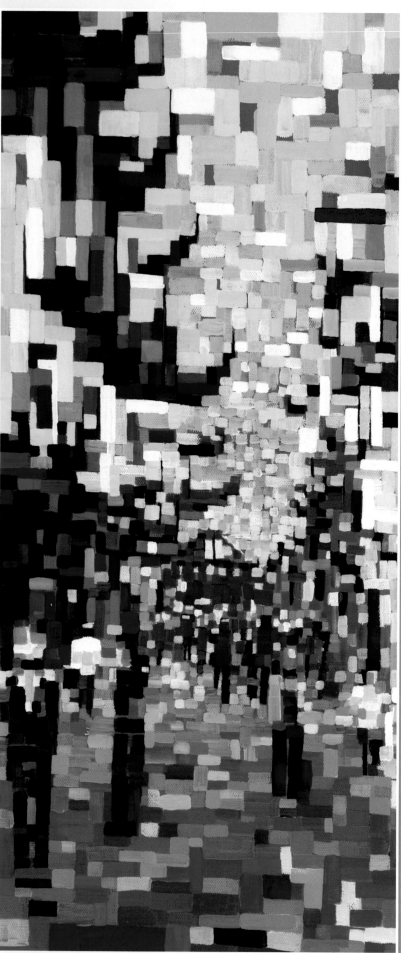

Venice landscapes

Explain to the children that they are going to work on an exciting project about cities. The first of three sections will be on the city of Venice, and they will be comparing Michelle Lovric's poem *A Young Rat Goes to Venice …* (page 42) with Agnes Treherne's watercolour illustration of the poem (page 43) to create their own scenes of the city.

Approach

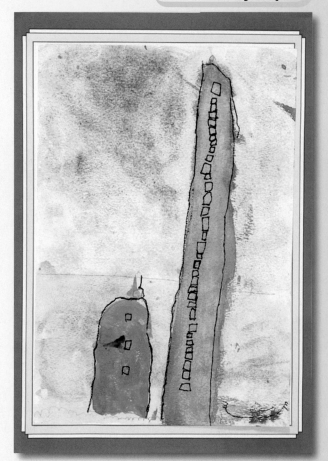

1   Show children a few images of the city of Venice and talk about its physical features, especially its canals, bridges and ancient buildings. Explain that they are going to sketch an image of Venice based on one of the ones you have shown them.

2   With the children read *A Young London Rat Goes to Venice …* by Michelle Lovric.

3   Ask the following questions: *What does the air smell of?* (salt, cake and sardines). *Which animal do the bridges remind the poet of?* (cats). *What does the young London rat see on the bridge above him?* (a Venice rat). *Can you remember what the two rats talk about in the poem?* (cheese, fleas, chocolate, cabbage and mud). *Where do the rats decide to live at the end of the poem?* (Venice). *What animal do the boats remind the poet of?* (horses)

4   Look at Agnes Treherne's illustration of the poem opposite and discuss the detail she has included and how her illustration reflects the poem perfectly. Ask questions such as: *What can you see in the illustration that reminds you of the poem? What is your favourite part of the illustration? Where can we see a candle in the illustration? How do we know that children live in some of the buildings? Where is the gold fish bowl? Who do you think is looking out of the window on the top lefthand side of the illustration? How do we know that the picture shows Venice at night?*

5   Ask the children to select an image of Venice that they like and carefully, using sketch pencils, complete a light sketch on watercolour paper.

6   Paint a background watercolour wash over the paper and leave to dry.

7   Using watercolours, add detail to the painting and allow it to dry.

8   Using a fine-line black pen, pick out details in the picture, then mount the images on coloured card.

Resources
- Copy of the poem *A Young London Rat Goes to Venice…* by Michelle Lovric
- Copy of Agnes Treherne's illustration of the poem
- Sketch pencils
- Watercolour paper
- Watercolour paints
- Paint brushes
- Fine-line black pens
- Coloured card

Venice cityscape

Taking Michelle Lovric's poem (page 42) as an inspiration, the children are going to use paint and a selection of 3D materials, to investigate perspective. They will be creating a group display with buildings in the background, a watery foreground with a bridge and other details.

Approach

1   Read a selection of non-fiction and fiction books about Venice, such as *This is Venice* by Miroslav Sasek and *The Year in the City* by Kathy Henderson, illustrated by Paul Howard (non-fiction), and *Olivia Goes to Venice* by Ian Falconer (fiction).

2   Read the poem *A Young London Rat Goes to Venice …* by Michelle Lovric. Focus on the similes she uses in her poem. Ask the children to think of their own similes to describe the city.

3   Discuss the lines where the poet compares the bridges to cats ('bridges, like cats, /are arching their backs'), and gondolas to horses ('rear their heads up like horses'). Create illustrations for the display inspired by the poem.

4   Put a colour wash over the display board and use pale pastel colours for the buildings.

5   Outline the buildings in the distance and their reflection in the water, using gold or copper paint.

6   Embellish with silver paper to show the sunlight.

7   Sponge-paint sketch-paper with black paint, cut out window shapes then glue them onto cream cartridge paper to create the buildings in the display.

8   Place painted 3D rolled cardboard along the bridge to give depth and to create a balustrade effect.

9   Using collage materials and an upside-down paper plate, make the cat's head.

10   Make the end of the gondola with a horse's head using collage materials.

11   Create a watery effect in the foreground with sponge painting and by gluing on different coloured pieces of cellophane.

Glossary

Simile: a figure of speech in which two things are compared using the word 'like' or 'as'.

Resources
- Large board for the display
- Selection of picture books about Venice
- Copy of the poem, *A Young London Rat Goes to Venice …* by Michelle Lovric
- Rolled pieces of cardboard
- Poster paints and brushes
- Silver paper
- Cartridge paper
- Sketch paper
- Collage materials
- Paper plate
- Sponges
- Different coloured cellophane

Venice poetry

For the final project on the theme of Venice, the children create a poem by mixing and grouping lines inspired by Michelle Lovric's poem (page 42) and Agnes Treherne's illustration (page 43).

Approach

1   Read the poem *A Young London Rat Goes to Venice ...* by Michelle Lovric and discuss how the poet uses a refrain in her poem.

2   Look at Agnes Treherne's illustration and compare it to the poem.

3   Give children strips of card in red, white and green (the colours of the Italian flag).

4   Sitting in a circle, ask children to write a descriptive line about Venice and place the strips of paper in a circle.

5   Order the lines and start grouping them into themes.

6   Using the interactive whiteboard, group the lines into themes with one theme for each verse.

7   Using the drafting process, create a poem with three verses and practise reading the poem aloud as a class.

8   Type the poem up on the computer and mount with coloured card.

Glossary

Refrain: a phrase, line or group of lines, that is repeated throughout the poem, usually after every stanza.

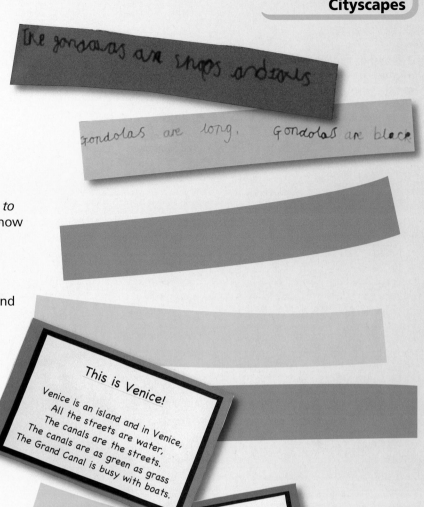

This is Venice!

Venice is an island and in Venice,
All the streets are water,
The canals are the streets.
The canals are as green as grass
The Grand Canal is busy with boats.

Gondolas are long! Gondolas are thin!
Gondolas are black!
Gondolas are gold!
The seats are red and comfy.
The gondolas are the shops and taxis.

Venice is flooded. The reflection is like
Two of the same thing.
Reflections are like paper.
The stars shine gorgeously!
I know you think it is a small city, but
actually it is beautiful.

Resources
- Copy of the poem, *A Young London Rat Goes to Venice ...* by Michelle Lovric
- Image of Agnes Treherne's illustration
- Strips of red, white and green card
- Pencils
- Computer
- Coloured card

Rio de Janeiro cityscape

The city of Rio de Janeiro offers a dramatic contrast to the historical watery maze that is Venice. Through creating a combination of artwork and poetry, the children can develop an understanding of the cityscape and architecture of this city.

Explain to the children that they are going to create a display and poem about the city Rio de Janeiro. The display will include the Sugar Loaf Mountain in the background, the buildings in the middle ground and the sand and sea in the foreground, and they will use Liz Chapman's Anonymous *Cityscapes* paintings (page 44) as an inspiration.

Approach

1   Look at a range of images of Rio de Janeiro and discuss the physical features of the city.

2   Look at Liz Chapman's *Cityscape* paintings and discuss how she has used shape and colour to make up her buildings.

3   Using a pencil, lightly indent polystyrene tiles with lots of vertical and horizontal lines, forming rectangles and squares.

4   Using a sponge roller, add paint to the tiles.

5   Press the painted side of the tile down onto A3 cartridge paper. Repeat with other printed tiles until the whole of the paper has been covered.

6   Colour photocopy the tile prints then cut out sections to create a collage cityscape of Rio de Janeiro.

7   Use different coloured poster paints for the sand and the sea.

8   Paint some trees in the background.

Resources
- Images of Rio de Janeiro
- Images of Liz Chapman's *Cityscape* paintings
- Square polystyrene tiles
- Pencils
- Poster paints and brushes
- Sponge rollers
- A3 cartridge paper
- Scissors

Cityscape poems

In her illustration (page 43) of the poem, *A Young London Rat Goes to Venice …*, Agnes Treherne includes many of the details from the poem, which helped her to visualise the scene.

For the second and final project exploring Rio de Janeiro, the children will be writing their own group poem in the style of Michelle Lovric's poem (page 42).

Approach

1 Read a range of poems about cities with the children before they start their own poetry writing.

2 Re-read Michelle Lovric's poem, *A Young London Rat Goes to Venice …*, and discuss why the poet uses a refrain at the end of the first stanza and at the end of the last stanza in her poem.

3 Show the children images of Rio de Janeiro and talk about the buildings and the cityscape; record a collection of words and phrases that describe the city.

4 Working in groups, give the children themes to work on: beach, climate, mountains and building, and encourage them to write their own lines of poetry about the topic.

5 As a class, share ideas and start writing a class poem, remembering to include a refrain.

Glossary

Refrain: a phrase, or a group of lines, that is repeated throughout the poem, usually after every stanza.

Stanza: two or more lines of poetry that together form one of the sections of a poem.

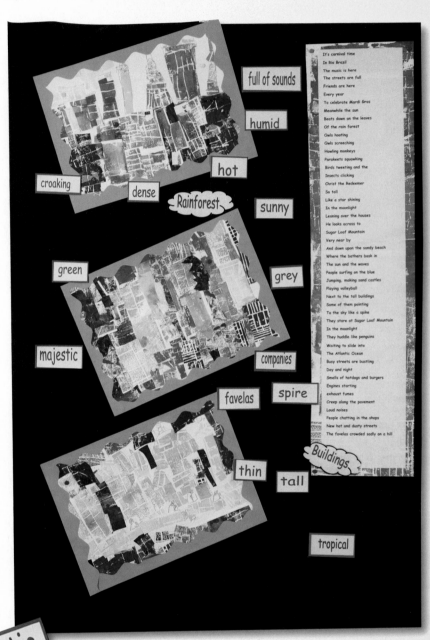

Resources
- Copy of the poem *A Young London Rat Goes to Venice …* by Michelle Lovric
- Image of Agnes Treherne's illustration of the poem
- Selection of poems about cities
- Paper and pencils
- Images of Rio de Janeiro cityscape

Cape Town cityscape

The South African city of Cape Town shares a number of features with the South American city of Rio de Janeiro. Cape Town is a city of contrasts. The coastline is very dramatic with vividly coloured sea and sand. The imposing presence of Table Mountain towers above the city.

Explain to the children that they will be creating a cityscape display of Cape Town, using inspiration from Liz Chapman's Anonymous *Cityscapes* paintings (page 44) and applying small blocks of colour. They will then prepare their own shape poems to add to the display.

Approach

1   Look at pictures of the city and discuss the physical features of Cape Town, focusing on Table Mountain.

2   Look at Liz Chapman's Anonymous *Cityscapes* paintings and discuss how she has used blocks of different colours to build up the scenes.

3   Cut A4 brown card into tile shapes.

4   Give children a selection of coloured card, tissue paper, pieces of felt and gold card and ask them to stick these on their tiles to depict the shape of Table Mountain. Encourage them to look carefully at images of the mountain.

5   Display the tiles.

6   Ask the children to work in pairs to make some buildings for the display by turning cardboard boxes inside out and painting them in bright colours.

7   Stick on black or white pieces of card for the windows.

8   Add the buildings to the display.

9   Using sponges and white paint, make sponge prints of clouds and add to the display with craft wire to create a 3D effect.

10 Embellish a large piece of bubble wrap with paint and glitter to represent the sea. Allow it to dry before placing on the display.

Resources

- Images of Cape Town and Table Mountain
- Images of Liz Chapman's Anonymous *Cityscapes* paintings
- Brown card
- Coloured card and gold card
- Tissue paper and pieces of felt
- Cardboard boxes
- Poster paints and paint brushes
- Glue
- Scissors
- Craft wire
- Sponges
- Glitter
- Bubble wrap

Cape Town shape poems

Explain to the children that to complete their display of Cape Town they are going to write poems in the shape of penguins to add to the sea section. Explain that penguins are often found in the waters of that area.

Approach

1 Look at some images of the South African penguins whose habitat is along the coastline of Cape Town. Discuss their appearance and the way they move.

2 Working as a class, make a collection of 'penguin words' for the children to use in their own poems.

3 Ask the children to choose and order their favourite words to use in their own poems.

4 Write five-lined poems using the following number of words in each line: 1, 2, 3, 4, and 5 to form a penguin shaped pieces of paper.

5 Write the shape poems onto penguin-shaped pieces of paper.

6 Display the poems on the Cape Town display, swimming across the water.

Glossary

Shape poems: poems where the text forms the same shape as the subject matter.

Resources
- Images of South African penguins
- Penguin shapes
- Pencils and paper

Dubai

Dubai is a unique and buzzing city with a mixture of modern and traditional buildings. There is an architectural mix of mosques, skyscrapers and, of course, the tallest building in the world (at the moment): the Burj Khalifa.

Explain to the children that they will be creating a display inspired by the Burj Khalifa and by Liz Chapman's paintings (page 44), then writing their own poems about the city.

Approach

1 Talk about the physical features of Dubai with the children, using photos as prompts; focus on its buildings and show them an image of the Burj Khalifa. Ask questions such as: *What is it like to live in Dubai? Why do you think Dubai has so many skyscrapers?*

2 Look at Liz Chapman's Anonymous *Cityscapes* paintings and talk about how she has focused on buildings. The backgrounds in her paintings are more blurred in contrast to the clarity of the foregrounds.

3 Get children to mix poster paints by adding a lighter colour to make softer tones.

4 Encourage children to work with two colours, mixing them together.

5 Using pencils, make brick-like marks on oblong polystyrene tiles.

6 Add colour to the polystyrene tiles by using a sponge roller and poster paint.

7 Build up different colours on the cartridge paper until each child has six different examples on their oblong tile prints.

8 Show the children an image of the Burj Khalifa on the whiteboard and draw its outline onto a roll of thick paper.

9 Place the A3 paper prints over the outline shape of the Burj Khalifa to decide where the colours should go on the display.

10 Cut the A3 printed papers in half and then cut into rectangular shapes.

11 Cover the bulk of the building with a collection of the printed shapes.

Resources
- Images of Dubai and the Burj Khalifa skyscraper
- Image of Liz Chapman's Anonymous *Cityscapes* paintings
- Oblong polystyrene tiles
- Pencils
- Poster paints and paint brushes
- Sponge roller
- A3 cartridge paper
- Roll of thick paper
- Scissors
- Glue

Dubai poetry

For the final project in this section, children will be writing a group poem about Dubai, using some of the methods that Michelle Lovric uses in her poem about Venice (page 42).

Approach

1 Read a selection of poems about cities, including *A Young London Rat Goes to Venice …* by Michelle Lovric, with the children and discuss Lovric's use of repetition, rhyme and alliteration.

2 Show the children images of the skyscrapers in Dubai.

3 Brainstorm words and poetic phrases that describe the physical features of Dubai.

4 Get the children to work in groups and write rhyming words and poetic lines that might be useful for their class poems about Dubai's cityscape.

5 Share ideas with the whole class and together create a chorus for the poem.

6 Using the drafting process, write a class poem around the children's ideas.

Glossary

Alliteration: the repetition of the same consonant sounds in words, often at the beginning of words.

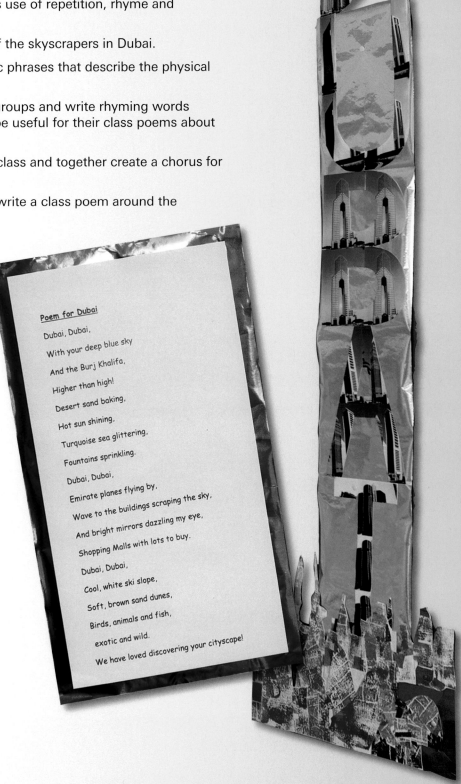

Poem for Dubai

Dubai, Dubai,
With your deep blue sky
And the Burj Khalifa,
Higher than high!
Desert sand baking,
Hot sun shining,
Turquoise sea glittering,
Fountains sprinkling.
Dubai, Dubai,
Emirate planes flying by,
Wave to the buildings scraping the sky,
And bright mirrors dazzling my eye,
Shopping Malls with lots to buy.
Dubai, Dubai,
Cool, white ski slope,
Soft, brown sand dunes,
Birds, animals and fish,
exotic and wild.
We have loved discovering your cityscape!

Resources

• Selection of rhyming poems and copy of *A Young London Rat Goes to Venice …* by Michelle Lovric
• Images of Dubai's cityscape
• Pencils and paper

London

Finally in this chapter, the focus shifts to the city of London. For the following six projects, children will be exploring this city using one poem and one painting as inspiration for poetry, colour and perspective.

Annie Freud has used the painting, *Liverpool Street* (opposite), by the artist Liz Chapman, as her inspiration for this poem. Both the poem and the painting reflect aspects of life in the City of London and capture its essence in different ways. To capture the atmosphere at first hand, Annie Freud went to the City to stand in the exact spot where Liz Chapman started her painting.

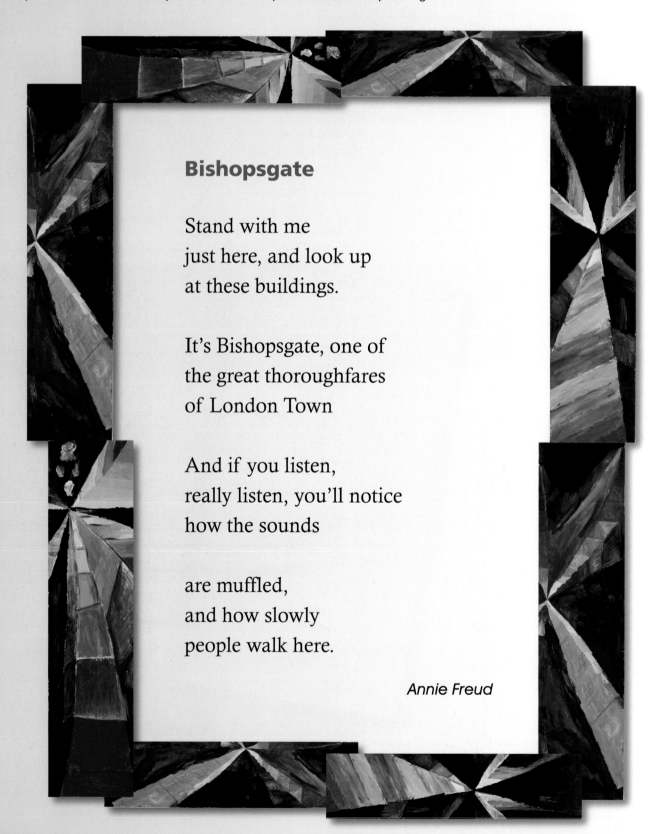

Bishopsgate

Stand with me
just here, and look up
at these buildings.

It's Bishopsgate, one of
the great thoroughfares
of London Town

And if you listen,
really listen, you'll notice
how the sounds

are muffled,
and how slowly
people walk here.

Annie Freud

Liverpool Street

In Liz Chapman's painting, *Liverpool Street*, two red buses are going in different directions in the foreground, a black taxi and a cyclist are heading towards us and there are people milling around. All the high-rise buildings tower over the lower Georgian and Victorian terraces, with the Gherkin dominating the skyline. As the sunlight strikes the buildings, they burst into colour.

City sketches

As preparation for her paintings, artist Liz Chapman always visits the places that she is going to paint. She takes photos of her chosen place from different perspectives, and sometimes makes notes of the colours she is seeing so she doesn't forget them.

Explain to the children that they are going to do some sketches of old and new buildings in a city setting, in preparation for a larger display piece.

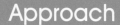
Approach

1   If you live in a city, use your own environment for this activity. If not, you could collect a selection of photos depicting old and new architecture in a city environment.

2   Ask children to choose buildings to sketch that will allow the final display to show a contrast between old and new architecture.

3   Look up at the buildings and observe the details from different perspectives or use photographs that provide a variety of perspectives.

4   Using a sketch pencil, draw one of the buildings, adding detail and focusing on the brickwork or exterior texture, the style of windows and overall shape.

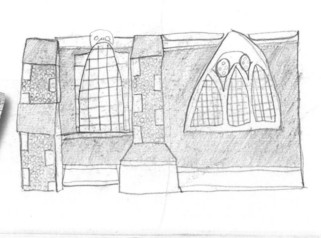

Resources
- Photos of old and new city architecture
- Ideas Books
- Sketch pencils
- A3 sketch paper

Tanka poetry

In her poem *Bishopsgate* (page 54), Annie Freud invites the reader to stand with her and look up at the elegant and timeless world of the City of London and the mood is a reflective one. The muffled sounds and slow-walking people evoke a rather hushed atmosphere in which the poet invites us to listen very carefully.

The second project in this chapter invites children to write their own poems about London, using Annie Freud's poem and Liz Chapman's painting (page 55) as well as their own city sketches for inspiration.

Approach

1   Read the poem *Bishopsgate* with the children and focus on how the poet invites us to join her and look at the City.

2   Explain to the children how the first line of the second stanza flows into the other two lines with no punctuation (enjambment), making it easier to read aloud. The use of full stops and commas in a poem is very important as it reinforces how the poet wants the poem to be read.

3   Look at Liz Chapman's painting *Liverpool Street* and discuss how closely Annie Freud has observed the details of the painting in her poem.

4   Read the poem again and ask questions such as: *How does the poem make you feel? Happy, calm, amazed? How does the poem relate to the painting? Why do you think the sounds are muffled?*

5   Discuss the children's city sketches (opposite) and how they reflect both ancient and modern architecture, which is a mix found in most cities.

6   Working with response partners, brainstorm ideas for writing poems on the subject of cityscapes that have a similar rhythm to *Bishopsgate*.

7   Encourage children to begin their poems by inviting the reader to look up at the buildings (those in Liz Chapman's painting), just as Annie Freud has done.

8   Encourage the children to consider carefully how the words are put together and remind them that every word counts. Older children could try to use the structure of a tanka poem.

9   Type up the poems and display them with the children's city sketches.

Glossary

Tanka: a form of Japanese poetry that has five lines with thirty-one syllables: 5, 7, 5, 7 and 7.

Resources

- Copies of the poem *Bishopsgate* by Annie Freud
- Ideas Books
- Image of *Liverpool Street* painting by Liz Chapman
- Pencils
- Computer

Cityscapes
The buildings are so high
Towering in the sky
Looming like giants
Reflecting the sunlight now
See them and know where you are

Whitehall
Towering here within
Whitehall are many different
Awe-striking mountains
Twisted steel; painted glass
Come, see them, and fall in love.

Colour mixing

In her paintings of cities Liz Chapman uses colour to create the illusion of space. Generally speaking, the paler the colour in a cityscape, the more distant the view will appear. Stronger, more vibrant colours are kept for the foreground and create the sense that they are closer to the viewer.

The following simple exercise teaches the children to control the amount and consistency of paint they use. The final results are beautiful in themselves but also act as a valuable colour code for the next cityscape project.

Approach

1   Ask the children to draw six squares across their paper and four squares up using a ruler.

2   Paint the square top left in orange and top right at the other end of the row in blue. These are complimentary colours and work best for this exercise.

3   Add a little of the blue to the orange and paint along the line of squares, adding paint to step the colour equally until the orange turns to blue.

4   After painting each individual square, ask the children to add a little water to their brush and lighten the original colour by mixing on a paper plate. Then start in the second square down on the left.

5   Get children to keep doing this along the rows from each original colour that they paint.

Resources
- Pencils
- Rulers
- Quality paper
- Paper plates (for mixing)
- Small soft brush
- Watercolours
- Water pots

Rules of perspective

Before moving on to the final project in this chapter – to create architectural style drawings of huge buildings – help children to understand basic rules of perspective with these drawings. This builds on the perspective element introduced to the Venice cityscape (page 46).

Approach

1. To create the horizon line, draw a horizontal line across A4 sketch paper and make a small cross in the centre. This depicts the vanishing point (drawing 1).

2. Draw a number of lines going through the vanishing point to the edges of the paper (drawing 2).

3. In the different sections on the paper, draw vertical lines that are parallel with the edges of the paper (drawing 3).

4. Add a number of angled lines to the remaining sections to create perspective (drawing 4).

①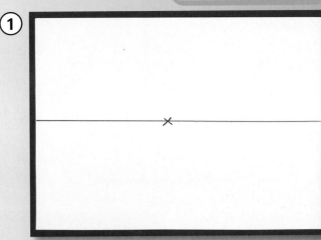

②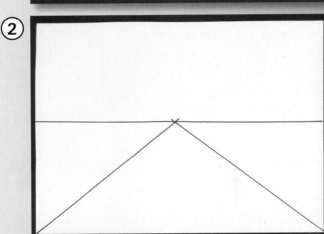

③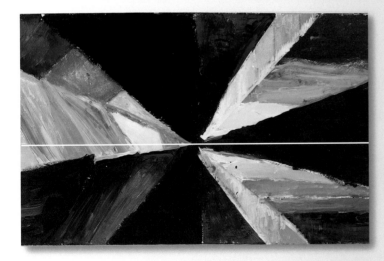

④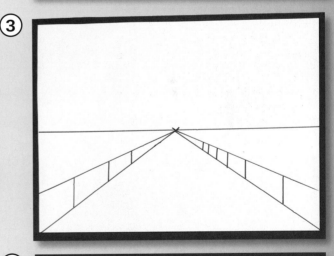

Glossary

Vanishing point: the point on the horizon where parallel lines appear to meet.

Resources
- A4 sketch paper
- Rulers
- Dark, sharp pencil
- Eraser

59

Architecture

One idea for starting this project could be to invite a local architect to come into school and talk with the children about the importance of designing buildings that are practical, fit for purpose and beautiful. As a focus for discussion, ask the architect to comment on Liz Chapman's painting, *Liverpool Street* (page 55), and Annie Freud's poem, *Bishopsgate* (page 54).

Explain to the children that they will be creating large, architectural-style paintings to reflect the towering buildings in the City of London.

Approach

1   Working from their perspective drawings (page 59), ask children to draw their perspective lines on large, narrow boards to fill the whole space.

2   Using the same colour mixing approach as on page 58, add colour to the different sections. Make sure that the more vibrant colours are kept in the foreground, remembering the techniques used by Liz Chapman in her paintings.

Resources
- Large, narrow boards
- Rulers
- Pencils
- Acrylic paints in blue, orange and white
- Paint brushes

Lines of architecture

In Liz Chapman's painting, *Liverpool Street* (page 55), all the high-rise buildings tower above the older buildings, giving us a greater sense of the area. The modern buildings are tall because there isn't much space and the modern materials reflect the wealth of the area.

For this project, the children will be adding buildings on top of their own city paintings.

Approach

1   Read Annie Freud's poem, *Bishopsgate* (page 54), and encourage the children to view their patchwork board backgrounds together as if they were on the pavement looking up at buildings that loom from above.

2   Look at the children's original city sketches (page 56) and use these as an inspiration for the next stage.

3   Using white acrylic paint, paint expressive lines on top of the patchwork board backgrounds to create smaller buildings.

4   To create an eye-catching display, place the patchwork boards closely together in a vertical position so that the viewer has to look up at them.

Resources

- White acrylic paint
- Small brushes
- Children's city sketches
- Children's large patchwork boards
- A copy of *Bishopsgate* by Annie Freud

5. Endings

Everyday things

The theme of this chapter is Endings, of different sorts. The children work through seven personal art projects which ask them to think for themselves about what 'Endings' mean to them, using the following two poems and artwork print for inspiration.

In this poem, *A World Without Endings*, Gareth P Jones plays around with everyday things like ice cream, playtime and a day at the beach. In the same way, printmaker Jo de Pear uses everyday objects to represent people's personalities (see opposite). Both for the poet and the artist a sense of an ending is very prevalent in their work.

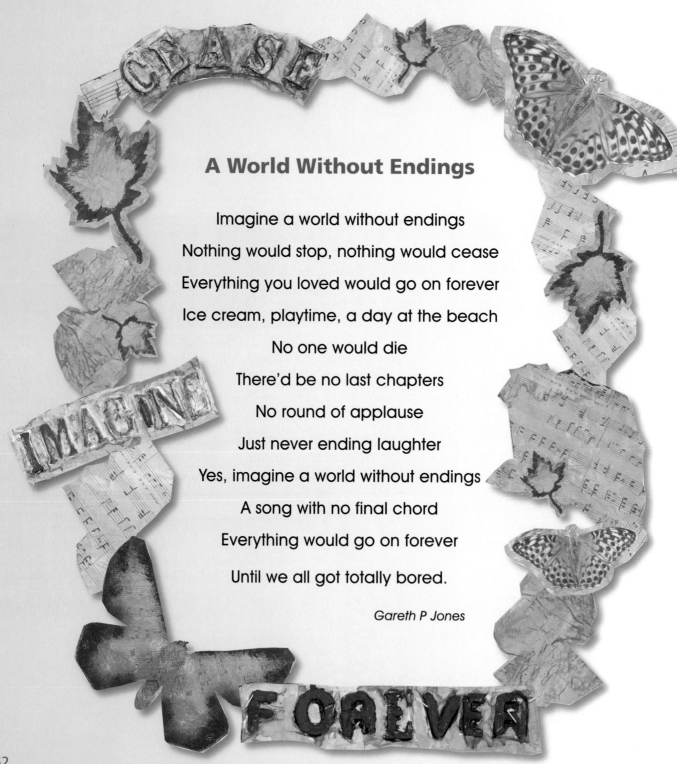

A World Without Endings

Imagine a world without endings

Nothing would stop, nothing would cease

Everything you loved would go on forever

Ice cream, playtime, a day at the beach

No one would die

There'd be no last chapters

No round of applause

Just never ending laughter

Yes, imagine a world without endings

A song with no final chord

Everything would go on forever

Until we all got totally bored.

Gareth P Jones

Portrait

In her print, *Portrait*, Jo de Pear has used various bits of cutlery inherited from female family members as her inspiration. For the artist, they seemed the perfect way of representing the person who owned them; she has arranged these spoons in a row, like a family portrait.

This poem, *Endgame*, by Gavin Bruce, plays with the many different meanings and uses of the word 'end'.

Gavin Bruce has chosen an interesting title for his thought-provoking poem, *Endgame*, to engage the reader. The poem becomes a quest for the boy to find out what was at the end of everything. He chose the title *Endgame* for two reasons. First because the boy solves the problem and finds the answer when he meets the girl, and second because the reader has to work out the double meaning of the words.

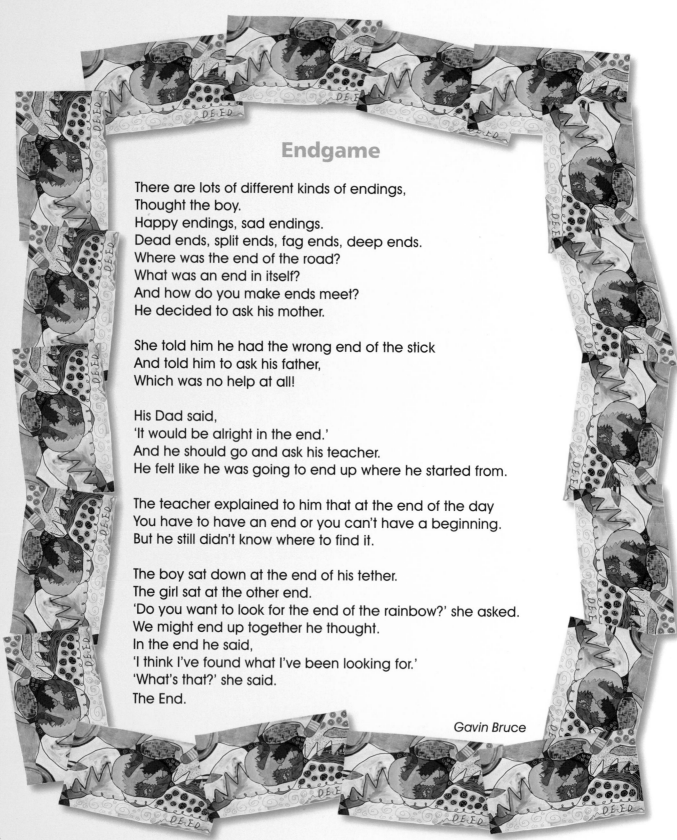

Endgame

There are lots of different kinds of endings,
Thought the boy.
Happy endings, sad endings.
Dead ends, split ends, fag ends, deep ends.
Where was the end of the road?
What was an end in itself?
And how do you make ends meet?
He decided to ask his mother.

She told him he had the wrong end of the stick
And told him to ask his father,
Which was no help at all!

His Dad said,
'It would be alright in the end.'
And he should go and ask his teacher.
He felt like he was going to end up where he started from.

The teacher explained to him that at the end of the day
You have to have an end or you can't have a beginning.
But he still didn't know where to find it.

The boy sat down at the end of his tether.
The girl sat at the other end.
'Do you want to look for the end of the rainbow?' she asked.
We might end up together he thought.
In the end he said,
'I think I've found what I've been looking for.'
'What's that?' she said.
The End.

Gavin Bruce

Drawings of everyday tools

For the first project, the children will be studying Jo de Pear's print (page 63) and how she uses everyday objects to represent deeper meanings. Working as a class, the children are going to make their own observational drawings of everyday objects that can be displayed together.

Approach

1   Look at the print, by Jo de Pear, and ask the children what they think it's about. Then tell them the title, *Portrait*. Does the title change their ideas about the image? What do they think the spoons might represent?

2   Read the information on page 63 and discuss how Jo de Pear has made a pictorial record of everyday objects that female members of her family used on a daily basis.

3   Ask the children to think about, and then discuss, everyday tools they are familiar with and how perhaps they associate them with someone in their family.

4   Arrange a selection of tools in the classroom and ask children to choose ones to draw.

5   Roll out a large piece of paper and create a class observational drawing using charcoal.

Resources
- Pencils
- Ideas Books
- Image of the print *Portrait* by Jo de Pear
- Large roll of paper
- Selection of tools
- Charcoal

Poetry

In his quirky poem, *A World Without Endings* (page 62), Gareth P Jones has chosen a thought-provoking title to engage the reader straight away. The poem has half rhymes ('cease' and 'beach', 'chapters' and 'laughter'), which give it more structure and rhythm when it's read aloud; the third from last line rhymes with the last line. Apart from a full stop at the end and three commas, there is no other punctuation in the poem; the commas make it more readable and the lack of full stops allows it to flow when read aloud.

For the second project, the children are going to write their own poems, using Gareth P Jones' poem and Jo de Pear's print (page 63) as inspiration.

Approach

1   Read the poem, *A World Without Endings,* with the children and discuss what the poet thinks a world without any ending would be like.

2   Discuss the structure of the poem and focus on the poet's use of repetition and rhyme.

3   Remind children how printmaker Jo de Pear uses everyday objects as an inspiration in her work.

4   Encourage the children to come up with their own examples of everyday objects or activities that would go on forever, if there were no endings. Suggest that they use a mind map to record their ideas.

5   Ask children to write their own four-lined poems using the first line of Gareth P Jones's poem as their first line and based on ideas recorded in their mind maps.

6   Prepare the poems for display.

Resources
- Copies of *A World Without Endings* poem by Gareth P Jones
- Image of print, *Portrait*
- Pencils
- A4 paper

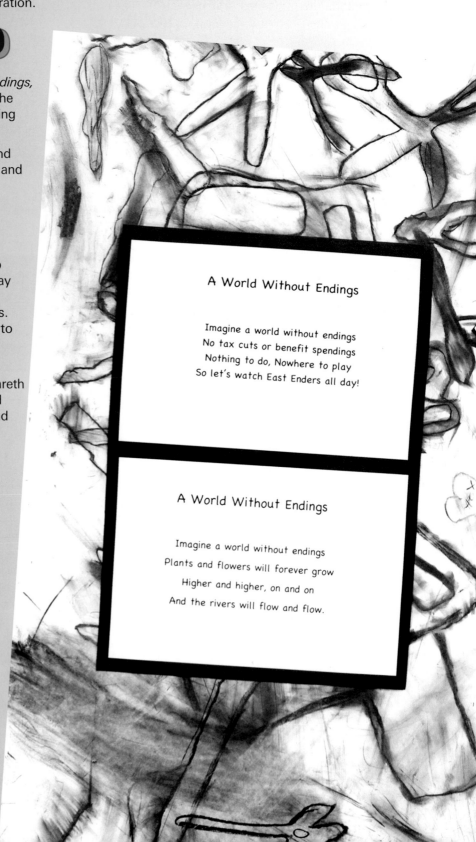

A World Without Endings

Imagine a world without endings
No tax cuts or benefit spendings
Nothing to do, Nowhere to play
So let's watch East Enders all day!

A World Without Endings

Imagine a world without endings
Plants and flowers will forever grow
Higher and higher, on and on
And the rivers will flow and flow.

Blind drawing mono prints

To produce her print (page 63), Jo de Pear made a rubbing from the surface of each spoon. She covered the spoon with paint and then gently rubbed fine tissue paper over the surface to get a very crude print. This helped to bring out the different characteristics of the spoons, like an impression.

Explain to the children that this next project is all about exploring with your eyes the object you are drawing before you make any mark on the paper. The drawing activity here enables children to produce a drawing with personality.

Approach

1   Roll black ink onto a plastic tray and place good quality paper on the inked surface of the tray.

2   Give the children a selection of natural objects to draw onto the back of the paper that is now lying on the ink-covered tray.

3   Using pencils with cardboard guides so that children cannot see their drawing, follow the outline of the object.

4   Create a continuous line drawing by not taking the pencil off the paper and add detail.

5   Carefully peel back the paper to reveal the mono print.

Resources
- Plastic trays
- Roller
- Black ink
- A5 sketch paper
- Selection of natural objects
- Pencils
- Guides (pieces of A5 card with a central hole for a pencil)

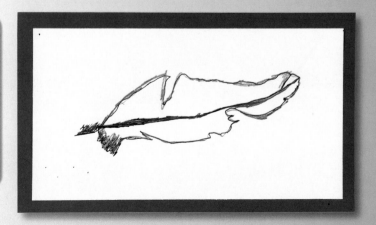

Mixed-media montage

The inspiration for this project came from a combination of visual- and process-based sources. Using the haunting imagery from Jo de Pear's prints (page 63) together with wow words taken from Gareth P Jones's poem (page 62), children can spend time deciding on the natural objects they could use to portray a sense of time passing, such as leaves, butterflies and feathers.

Approach

1 Give the children a plain board to work on. Ask them to cut out pictures of feathers, insects or keys, position them on the board and then glue them down.

2 Choose a wow word from the poem, then glue the word as 3D letters on the board.

3 Stick small pieces of white tissue paper over the whole board. Using a brush, cover the letters and tissue paper with watered-down PVA glue.

4 Tear sheets of musical scores out and glue onto the tissue paper.

5 Use watercolour pencils to make the letters look more 3D.

6 Use a brown wash over the surface of the work, making sure not to cover the letters.

7 Using the watercolour pencils, draw over the images that need to be highlighted.

8 Choose a stencil shape and place it on the composition and, with undiluted poster paint and a hard brush, stipple the stencil design onto the board.

9 Display the artwork with some of the poems the children created based on *A World Without Endings*.

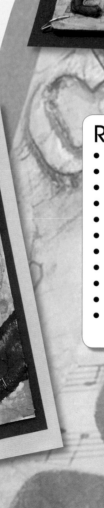

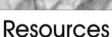

Resources

- Pictures of leaves, keys and insects
- Boards in different sizes
- 3D letters
- Tissue paper
- Scissors
- PVA glue and hard brushes
- Musical scores
- Water colour pencils
- Acrylic or poster paints
- Watered-down brown poster paint
- Stencils of leaves, feathers, keys and butterflies

What's at the end of a line?

For this project, children will be considering the poem *Endgame* (page 64) by Gavin Bruce, and producing a visual representation of his ideas.

Approach

1 Read the poem, *Endgame*, by Gavin Bruce and highlight the phrases that include the word 'end'.

2 Get the children to think of pictures that could convey the meaning of the words and discuss their ideas.

3 Give children a sheet of white A4 card and ask them to glue on an image of a child blowing bubbles.

4 Using the children's ideas about the phrases in the poem, ask them to use various mediums to draw contrasting lines – as if they were being blown across the page.

5 Add some of the words or phrases from the poem and integrate these with pictures linked to the poem.

6 Children can use a variety of mediums to create a colourful composition.

Resources

- Copy of *Endgame* by Gavin Bruce
- A4 white card
- Images of children blowing bubbles
- Pencils
- Pens
- Watercolours and paint brushes
- Pastels

Endgame poetry

Turn to Gavin Bruce's poem (page 64) and explain to the children that the poet's use of repetition in the fourth line conveys a powerful image of everyday things that are quite different from one another and also have more than one meaning. Dialogue is used effectively at the end of the poem to bring it to a satisfactory conclusion.

For the penultimate project in this chapter, children are going to use their ideas from the previous projects and Gavin Bruce's poem to write their own class poem about endings.

Approach

1   Read *Endgame* by Gavin Bruce again with the children and discuss some of the phrases containing the word 'end'.

2   Look at Jo de Pear's print, *Portrait*, on page 63 and discuss how she uses everyday objects in her work to depict a sense of an ending.

3   Look at the *What's at the End of the Line?* artworks on page 69 and create another image freely using words, lines and colour to depict the essence of the poem.

4   In groups, ask the children to create tableaux where a moment from the poem is captured.

5   Do some hot seating where one child takes on the part of one of the characters in the poem and the other children ask questions.

6   Divide the class into two groups and ask each group to pass around a piece of paper with the heading 'Endgame' with each child in turn adding one line. All the lines need to be about the theme of Endings and must link together seamlessly to create communal poems.

7   Working with response partners, give each pair a copy of their group poem and use the drafting process to change some of the words for more expressive choices, if necessary.

8   Read the group poems aloud and comment with the children on their effectiveness.

Game Over!

The notes go on forever,
When will they end?
In a spiral of time.
There can be no beginning
If you can't find the end!
When the night ends,
The day begins.
The end of the rainbow
Is the start of a fortune.
Game Over!

Resources

- Copies of the poem *Endgame* by Gavin Bruce
- Image of the print *Portrait* by Jo de Pear
- Whiteboards, pens and erasers
- A3 sheets of paper and pencils

String words

Explain to the children that Gavin Bruce has used everyday phrases in his poem *Endgame* (page 64) to get them to think about their true meaning.

For the final project in this chapter, children will be producing decorative word pictures, using words and phrases from the poem that they feel capture its essence.

Approach

1   Read the poem *Endgame* by Gavin Bruce and select words or short phrases that reflect the essence of the poem.

2   Give children a selection of string, wool and ribbon to choose from.

3   Using black card as a background, form words from the poem using cursive writing to create large, decorative words.

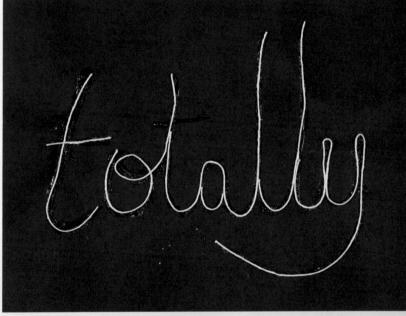

Resources

- Copy of *Endgame* by Gavin Bruce
- String
- Wool
- Glue
- Ribbon
- Black card
- Scissors

71

The Apple Tree poems (page 30).

A World Without Endings (shown in part on page 68).